FRIENDS OF COLLEGE LIBRARIES

CLIP Note #9

Compiled by
Ronelle K. H. Thompson
Director, Mikkelsen Library
Augustana College, Sioux Falls, South Dakota

College Library Information Packet Committee
College Libraries Section
Association of College and Research Libraries
A division of the American Library Association 1987

Published by the Association of College and
Research Libraries, a division of the
American Library Association
50 East Huron Street
Chicago, Illinois 60611

ISBN 0-8389-7171-7

The paper used in this publication meets the minimum
requirements of American National Standard for
Information Sciences--Permanence of Paper for Printed
Library Materials, ANSI Z39.48-1984. ∞

Copyright © 1987 by the American Library Association.
Portions of this publication may be photocopied for the
noncommercial purpose of scientific or educational
advancement granted by Sections 107 and 108 of the
Copyright Revision Act of 1976.

Printed in the United States of America

TABLE OF CONTENTS

INTRODUCTION 1

CLIP NOTES SURVEY (RESULTS) 5

CONSTITUTIONS

    Robert Frost Library 17
    Amherst College
    Amherst, Massachusetts

    Howard Colman Library 19
    Rockford College
    Rockford, Illinois

    Margaret and Herman Brown Library 22
    Abilene Christian University
    Abilene, Texas

    Jessie Ball DuPont Library 25
    The University of the South
    Sewanee, Tennessee

    Charles Leaming Tutt Library 27
    Colorado College
    Colorado Springs, Colorado

BY-LAWS

    Robert Frost Library 33
    Amherst College
    Amherst, Massachusetts

    Howard Colman Library 37
    Rockford College
    Rockford, Illinois

    Ashland College Library 38
    Ashland College
    Ashland, Ohio

    Crosby Library 42
    Gonzaga University
    Spokane, Washington

    Folke Bernadotte Memorial Library 45
    Gustavus Adolphus College
    St. Peter, Minnesota

    Swarthmore College Libraries 53
    Swarthmore College
    Swarthmore, Pennsylvania

MEMBERSHIP BROCHURES

    Iris Holt McEwen Library 59
    Elon College
    Elon College, North Carolina

    Ashland College Library 60
    Ashland College
    Ashland, Ohio

    Swarthmore College Libraries 62
    Swarthmore College
    Swarthmore, Pennsylvania

    Mary Norton Clapp Library 65
    Occidental College
    Los Angeles, California

    Parkside Library 68
    University of Wisconsin - Parkside
    Kenosha, Wisconsin

    William Luther Cobb Library 71
    Eckerd College
    St. Petersburg, Florida

    Boyd Lee Spahr Library 74
    Dickinson College
    Carlisle, Pennsylvania

    Oberlin College Library 79
    Oberlin College
    Oberlin, Ohio

PROGRAM IDEAS

    Shadek-Fackenthal Library 91
    Franklin and Marshall College
    Lancaster, Pennsylvania

    Swarthmore College Libraries 93
    Swarthmore College
    Swarthmore, Pennsylvania

    Watkinson Library 95
    Trinity College
    Hartford, Connecticut

    Margaret Clapp Library 98
    Wellesley College
    Wellesley, Massachusetts

    Connecticut College Library 99
    Connecticut College
    New London, Connecticut

NEWSLETTERS

    Jessie Ball DuPont Library 107
    The University of the South
    Sewanee, Tennessee

    Schaffer Library 111
    Union College
    Schenectady, New York

    Everett Needham Case Library 115
    Colgate University
    Colgate, New York

    Margaret Clapp Library 119
    Wellesley College
    Wellesley, Massachusetts

    Robert Frost Library 123
    Amherst College
    Amherst, Massachusetts

PUBLICATIONS

    Goddard Library 127
    Clark University
    Worcester, Massachusetts

    Schaffer Library 128
    Union College
    Schenectady, New York

    Everett Needham Case Library 130
    Colgate University
    Colgate, New York

    Connecticut College Library 132
    Connecticut College
    New London, Connecticut

BIBLIOGRAPHY..134

INTRODUCTION

Objective of the Study

The College Library Information Packet Notes program provides "college and small university libraries with state-of-the-art reviews and current documentation on library practices and procedures of relevance to them." This CLIP Notes publication is intended to increase the number and strengthen the efforts of college library friends groups at a time when many college libraries face critical financial needs.

Background

Library friends groups have long been popular support groups for public libraries. The reasons such support groups develop for the local public library are obvious--parents bring their children to storytimes, the business community finds needed background information, and teachers obtain print and nonprint materials to support their classroom efforts.

It is more difficult to identify the interested people needed to establish and maintain an active support group for a college library. The obvious constituency--alumni--frequently do not live nearby, making associated programs and benefits of membership less desirable to them. Further, many community residents may already be involved in a public library support group, or do not perceive that an academic library needs their support.

Declining enrollments are making it increasingly difficult for many institutions to increase and sometimes to maintain their library's share of general operating funds. With the costs for library services tied to increasingly expensive information, it has become essential for college librarians to look beyond their institution's operating budget for additional funds. Library friends programs are a means to retain and develop alumni and community interest in and support for the activities of the library and the institution. The annual dues income from a friends group is a useful source of funds. Andrew Eaton points out the possibility, however, that "more important in the long run is the opportunity provided by the organization to acquaint bookish and/or wealthy friends with the library's role and needs" (356).

Although, according to Scott Bennett, there is no reliable historical account of the development of friends groups (26), Gwyn, McArthur, and Furlow discovered that the earliest friends group started in 1923 (272). The oldest college library friends group responding to this ACRL CLIP Notes survey was formed in 1937. Clearly, there are well-established college library friends groups. The gathering together in one place of materials from existing college library friends groups will make it possible for those groups to adapt ideas from each other and provide background information to library friends groups still in the planning stages of development.

Librarians working with friends groups or forming such a support group may seek assistance from Friends of Libraries U.S.A. (FOLUSA), a nonprofit organization affiliated with the American Library Association. FOLUSA's major objectives are to help new Friends of Libraries groups form and to encourage the development of established groups.

The author acknowledges the cooperation of all the college librarians who, in responding to this survey, have shared their experiences in establishing and maintaining local friends groups. Their willingness to describe their experiences has resulted in a CLIP Notes publication that will be useful to their colleagues across the country. Indeed, as Edward Holley states, librarians must assume the primary task of interpreting the library to those who have resources to give (11).

Survey Process

The published literature on college library friends groups was reviewed and a questionnaire developed. The questionnaire was mailed in February 1987 to the 187 libraries that have agreed to cooperate with CLIP Notes surveys. The colleges surveyed included those institutions defined by the Carnegie Council on Policy Studies in Higher Education in 1976 as either Comprehensive Universities and Colleges I or Liberal Arts Colleges I. In addition to completing the questionnaire, those libraries with friends groups were asked to supply copies of their group's by-laws or organizational structure, promotional literature, newsletters, brochures, and sample projects or programs. The returned questionnaires were tabulated using SPSS (Statistical Package for the Social Sciences) and accompanying materials evaluated for inclusion in this publication.

Survey Results

Of the 187 surveys mailed, 136 were returned, or 73%, by April 1987. The survey asked participating librarians to describe their libraries generally, whether they had a friends group, and, if they did have a friends group, to describe its organization and function. If no friends group was present, librarians were asked under what circumstances they might consider beginning such an organization.

Libraries with Friends Groups (Questions B.8 - C.19)

Only 33 of the 136 (24%) libraries responding to our survey had friends groups specifically associated with their college library. The library staff was clearly the most active group in the formation of these friends organizations. There appears to be no correlation in our survey sample between the size of a college, as indicated by enrollment, and whether or not it has a library friends group. The college friends groups responding had founding dates for their organizations ranging from 1937 to 1987. Membership levels were weighted in the 50-300 member range, with the largest friends group in the survey having 704 members. Most of the friends groups responding have an annual membership fee, but they have a wide variety of categories and associated contribution levels. The majority of the college friends groups surveyed have a governing board that includes representatives from the college administration, library staff, faculty, alumni, and community. Some of these groups also include student representatives on their friends board. Although their general membership includes all of the previously-mentioned constituents, alumni and community members represent the largest percentage of membership.

Activities of Friends Groups   (Questions D.20 - 26)

Although most college library friends groups work closely with library staff, almost a third of the respondents indicated that friends activities are planned and implemented independent of the library. The majority of college library friends groups indicated that the most important purpose of their organization was to raise funds and/or gifts in kind for the library. The list of projects completed, whether fund-raising in nature or not, is fascinating. Clearly, the library groups responding have been creative in their efforts to support their libraries financially and to provide cultural programs for their membership.

While almost all of the responding friends groups raise more than $1000 each year, the breakdown of groups raising monies in the other three categories--$1000-$5000, $5000-$10,000, or $10,000-up--is fairly evenly distributed. Most friends groups have to pay for all their operating expenses (copying, postage, etc.) from the funds they raise. Less than a third of the groups had a development office staff member from the college assigned to them.

Libraries without Friends Groups   (Questions E.27 - 28)

Surveys were returned from 103 libraries that do not have an active friends group. Some of those respondents indicated that a previous friends group was now defunct. Other responses indicated a wide disparity of opinions about the value of such a support group. Some respondents acknowledged an interest in forming a friends group, but indicated insufficient time to organize one. Others felt that such groups required too much library staff time for the amount of money raised. Between these strong opinions were those who cited active public library friends groups already in the community, college fund-raising that met the needs of the library adequately in other ways, and friends groups for the college as a whole.

Respondents indicated that the single most important motivator for beginning a friends group would be a need for additional funds for the library, followed by pressure from the administration. It is interesting to note that five respondents are currently planning friends groups for their libraries.

Summary

The number of friends groups represented in this survey sample is comparatively small. However, these support groups appear to be strong organizations as evidenced by their survey answers and the descriptive materials they supplied. Included in this publication are examples of related materials of college library friends groups, such as constitutions, by-laws, membership brochures, program ideas, newsletters, and publications. Descriptions of size, color, and format of some of these materials are also included.

WORKS CITED

Bennett, Scott. "Library Friends: A Theoretical History." In Organizing the Library's Support: Donors, Volunteers, Friends. Ed. D. W. Krummel. Urbana-Champaign: U of Illinois, 1980. 23-32.

Eaton, Andrew J. "Fund Raising for University Libraries." College and Research Libraries 32 (1971): 351-61.

Gwyn, Ann, Anne McArthur, and Karen Furlow. "Friends of the Library." College and Research Libraries 36 (1975): 272-82.

Holley, Edward G. "The Library and Its Friends." In Organizing the Library's Support: Donors, Volunteers, Friends. Ed. D. W. Krummel. Urbana-Champaign: U of Illinois, 1980. 9-22.

Morein, P. Grady. "What is a CLIP Note?" College and Research Libraries News 46 (1985): 226.

Carnegie Council on Policy Studies in Higher Education. A Classification of Higher Education. Rev. ed. Berkeley: The Carnegie Foundation for the Advancement of Teaching, 1976.

CLIP NOTES SURVEY

FRIENDS OF COLLEGE LIBRARIES

Directions

This survey is being used to determine the activities in which friends groups associated with college libraries are engaged, how they are organized, and how effective they are.

A. General Information

1. Name of Library: _____

2. Name of Institution: _____

3. Address: _____
   _____

4. Number of full-time equivalent (FTE) students enrolled during fall 1986:

    126 Responses: Range 360 to 6247; Mean 2428.2; Median 2100

5. Number of full-time equivalent (FTE) faculty as of fall 1986:

    119 Responses: Range 28 to 733; Mean 156.7; Median 143

6. Number of full-time equivalent (FTE) librarians working in library as of fall 1986:

    131 Responses: Range 1 to 50; Mean 8.2; Median 7

7. Number of book volumes in collection:

    130 Responses: Range 100,000 to 1,002,000; Mean 263,700; Median 224,000

B. Friends Group Information: General

8. Does your library have a friends group?

    a) If yes, please answer questions #9-26

    b) If no, please answer questions #27-28

    136 Responses: 33 - Yes; 103 - No

C. Friends Group Information: Membership

9. Rank on a scale of 1-5 those groups involved in starting a friends organization for your library: (1 is very involved, 5 is least involved, use NA for no involvement)

    29 Responses

    5 ranked #1 ___College administration

    21 ranked #1___Library staff

    1 ranked #1 ___Faculty

    1 ranked #1 ___Alumni

    1 ranked #1 ___Community members (residents of the community with no other connection to college)

    Not ranked #1___Other: President's wife
    Library administration
    Trustees
    Previous Library Benefactors
    University Board of Regents

10. When was your friends group founded:

    32 Responses: Range 1937 to 1987; Mean 1970; Median 1975

11. What is the current membership of your friends group:

    33 Responses; Largest 704 members

    2___Less than 50 members

    11___50-150 members

    11___150-300 members

    6___300-500 members

    3___More than 500 members; How many members? 551, 665, 704

12. Does your friends group have membership fees:

    42 Responses

    14___Basic membership yearly, amount - Range $2.00 to $35.00; Mean $17.40; Median $15.00
    24___Levels of membership yearly - Range for all respondents $1.00 to $3,000.00
    4___No membership fees

13. Do you have special categories of membership to recognize significant contributions (i.e. life membership)?

    33 Responses

    23 ___Yes; If yes, list the categories and requirements

    10 ___No

    Categories and requirements included:

    Honorary Life: special guests, significant gift or endowment
    Life: elected by Board of Directors, $2500, $1000, $500, $200
    President's Fellow: $1000
    Foundation: $1000
    Patron: $500, $250, $150, $100, $50
    Sustaining: $500, $100, $50
    Sponsor: $300, $100
    Benefactor: $100
    Contributing: $100, $50, $25
    Active: $35, $25, $15
    Family: $30, $25, $20
    Individual: $20, $15, $10
    Student: $10, $5

14. If your friends group has a governing board, are all members eligible for board membership?

    28 Responses

    27 ___Yes

    1 ___No; If no, who is excluded: No answer provided

15. If your friends group has a governing board, indicate the number of board members in each of the following categories:

    ___College administrators
    11 Responses: Range 1 to 4; Mean 1.5; Median 1
    ___Library staff
    24 Responses: Range 1 to 4; Mean 1.8; Median 2
    ___Faculty
    19 Responses: Range 1 to 9; Mean 2.5; Median 2
    ___Students
    3 Responses: All responded 1
    ___Alumni
    18 Responses: Range 1 to 9; Mean 4.7; Median 3.5
    ___Community members
    20 Responses: Range 1 to 9; Mean 6; Median 6
    ___Other (please explain)
    2 Responses: University staff
                 Retired faculty

16. How often does the board meet and for how long?

    22 Responses: All but one meet for less than a half day; one meets for a weekend annually

17. How are the board members chosen?

    26 Responses

    2 ___General election by membership from slate nominated by general membership

    13___General election by membership from slate nominated by membership committee

    6___Volunteers

    5___indicated an additional "other"
    -by invitation
    -election by Board from slate nominated by membership committee

18. What is the length of the term for board members?

    24 Responses: Range 1 year to undefined; Mean 3.3; Median 3; 4 indicated length of term was undefined

19. Indicate the approximate percentage of the total friends membership represented by each of the following groups: (Your answers should total 100%)

    ___College administrators
    24 Responses: Range 1% to 12%; Mean 4.7%; Median 5%

    ___Library staff
    23 Responses: Range 1% to 20%; Mean 5.3%; Median 4%

    ___Faculty
    27 Responses: Range 1% to 60%; Mean 11.7%; Median 6%

    ___Students
    10 Responses: Range 1% to 20%; Mean 4.5%; Median 2.5%

    ___Alumni
    27 Responses: Range 5% to 92%; Mean 48.2%; Median 45%

    ___Community members
    28 Responses: Range 4% to 85%; Mean 35.5%; Median 31%

    ___Other (please explain)
    2 Responses: Range 2% to 10%; Mean 6%; Median 6%
    Included: Interested scholars

D. Friends Group Information: Activities

20. What is the relation of your friends group to the library: (check all that apply)

    33 Responses

    21___Library provides leadership for friends activities

    13___Library staff member assigned to friends group

    10___Friends activities are planned and implemented independent of the library

    3___Other (please explain)
       Board considers program ideas
       Friends funds used for lectures, special book purchases
       Members receive newsletter

21. Rank on a scale of 1-4 the following purposes of your friends group: (1 indicates most important purpose, 4 indicates least important purpose)

    30 Responses

    13 ranked #1___To raise funds and/or gifts in kind for support of library acquisitions

    17 ranked #1___To raise funds and/or gifts in kind for support of special library needs

    4 ranked #1___To provide special events/programs for membership

    7 ranked #1___To increase awareness of library as a resource for membership

    2 ranked #1___Other (please explain):
        -to purchase special collections or support special programs at library director's direction
        -to raise funds in support of general library needs
        -to publish library bulletin

22. Briefly list examples of projects undertaken by your friends group in the past two years. If any of these projects were fund-raising activities, include the amount raised.

    Fund-raising projects included:

     Books sales - $3000, $1800, $1600, $600, $400
       Friday afternoon book sales - $2000 over 9 months
       Used religious book sale - $1300
       St. Lucia Day book sale - $4000

Antiquarian Book Fair -$1000
Sale of early publications - $135
Sale of book bags with friends logo - profit not available
Rummage sales - $8000
Royale Affair, silent-live auction - $74,000
Birthday Club - $250
Fund raising dinner - $5000, $3000
"Mad Hatter's Tea Party" - $1800
125th anniversary dinner - $6000
Christmas Ball - $12,000
May Luncheon - $7000
Inaugural lecture and membership drive - $4000
Sponsorship of endowed funds - $61,063
Procurement of special collection - $20,000
Gifts in kind - $2000

Non-Fund-raising projects included:

Book and author dinner
Receptions - special events: Homecoming
Dinners/Dinner Programs
Luncheons
  (6-7 per year)
  Annual
Books and coffee
Tea to honor college authors
Open house to view Board member's collection of rare books
Symposium
Seminars
Book Collecting workshop
Lectures
  Literary luminaries
  Alumni
Author talks
Contributing to Book Arts lecture
Sponsored roundtable discussion of life of major library donor
Dramatic presentations
Chamber Music recitals
Cultural programs
Displays/Exhibits
  Association of American University Presses 1985 Book Show Awards
  Hard-Boiled Detective Fiction
  French Engraving Today
  Original Posters of the 1890's
  Leonard Baskin: His Graphic Arts
Library tours of other special academic libraries in region
Theater excursion
Sponsor study group on Soviet-American relations
Seminar on the art and craft of the book
Two short courses offered in January
Preparation and funding for informative library brochures

Purchase of directional signs for library
Partial financial support for summer reading programs
   for community and faculty children
Sponsor a library staff member's trip to professional
   meeting
Manage library display program
Manage local newspaper publicity
Stress history of library
Robert Frost Library Fellowship
Sponsorship of students book prizes
Scholarships to outstanding student workers
Student book centers
Publication of newsletter
Celebration of 50th anniversary of friends group
Celebration of 25th anniversary of library
Membership drive
Maintenance and planning of a garden area by library
"Friend for a Day" designation
International competition of new book plate

23. How much money was raised, including gifts in kind, by your friends group in each of the past two fiscal years:

    26 Responses

    1984-85   2 ___$ 0-1000

               9 ___$ 1000-5000

               6 ___$ 5000-10,000

               9 ___$ 10,000-up

    30 Responses

    1985-86   2 ___$ 0-1000

              12 ___$ 1000-5000

               8 ___$ 5000-10,000

               8 ___$ 10,000-up

24. What is the amount and the source of funds for the current operating budget (postage, copying, etc.) of your friends group:

    16 Responses (amount)
    Amount: Range $25.00 to $20,000; Mean $4049;
             Median $1717

    31 Responses (source)
     3 ___College funds through development office
     6 ___College funds through library
    21 ___Friends must raise all funds for miscellaneous
          expenses

25. Does the college development office have a staff member assigned to your friends group?

    32 Responses

    9 ___Yes; if yes, approximate number of hours spent/week on friends activities: Range 1 hour to 3 hours; Mean .4 hours; Median 0

    23 ___No

26. Would you start a friends group for your college library if you did not already have one?

    31 Responses

    30 ___Yes

    1 ___No; If no, why not? "Unless had support of the Development Office"

E. Libraries without Friends Groups

27. Rank on a scale of 1-5 the following reasons why your library does not have a friends group: (1 is most important reason, 5 is least important reason)

    60 Responses

    5 ranked #1 ___We had a friends group but it is now defunct

    25 ranked #1 ___We are interested, but have not had time to organize such a group

    21 ranked #1 ___No interest on part of library staff in organizing

    5 ranked #1 ___No support from alumni/community members in organizing

    19 ranked #1 ___No interest on part of college administration in organizing

    6 ranked #1 ___Public library in community already has a strong friends organization

    31 ranked #1 ___Other (please explain):

    1   Believe in "constituency" fund-raising
    4   Receive funds from university-wide friends groups
    5   Currently planning a friends group
    4   Do not wish to interfere with existing friends groups
    2   Strong ties with development office preclude need
    1   Active alumni and foundation groups on campus

3	Administration discourages individual fund-raising
1	Administration support precludes need
2	Development Office discourages individual friends groups
2	Formation of friends groups prohibited
2	Never thought of it
2	Too many friends groups exist in community
4	Too time-consuming
1	Not considered a priority
1	Organization of library network makes process complex
3	Not cost effective
1	All fund-raising focused through Development Office
1	Other methods of fund-raising more effective
1	Competes with Development Office
1	"Visiting Committee" helps in securing funds

28. Rank 1-5 the following as to their effectiveness in motivating you to begin a friends group for your college library: (1 is most important reason, 5 is least important reason)

   76 Responses

   22 ranked #1___Pressure from administration

   38 ranked #1___Need for additional funds for library

   8 ranked #1 ___Source of ideas/support for friends programming

   11 ranked #1___Willing library staff member to volunteer to serve as coordinator

   18 ranked #1___Other (please explain):

1	Pressure from college trustee
3	Non-staff member able to head organization
1	Workshop on friends groups
1	Support from alumni and community
1	Strengthen ties with community
1	New building - 1985
1	New director - 1986
1	Adequate staffing
1	Pressure from outside group
2	Need for such a group
1	Demand by alumni
3	Would not consider
1	Change in institutional policy
1	Good public relations
1	Administrative support and approval
1	Director believes in value of friends
1	Nucleus of group that would not interfere with public library

Person completing survey

    Name_____

    Title_____

    Date_____

_____ Please check if you would like a summary of the survey results.

IF YOUR COLLEGE LIBRARY HAS A FRIENDS GROUP, PLEASE INCLUDE REPRESENTATIVE COPIES OF ITS ORGANIZATIONAL STRUCTURE OR BY-LAWS, MISSION STATEMENT, PROMOTIONAL LITERATURE, NEWSLETTERS, BROCHURES, SAMPLE PROJECTS OR PROGRAMS.

CONSTITUTIONS

Revised 4/26/80

FRIENDS OF THE AMHERST COLLEGE LIBRARY

CONSTITUTION

ARTICLE I - NAME

The name of this association shall be Friends of the Amherst College Library (hereinafter called "Friends").

ARTICLE II - PURPOSES

The purposes of the Friends are to promote and further the interests of the Amherst College Library (hereinafter called "Library"), to serve as a medium for encouraging gifts and bequests to Amherst College of books and manuscripts and of funds for needs beyond the Library budget, to encourage interest in books, printing, bibliography and book collecting and generally to increase the usefulness, facilities and resources of the Library.

ARTICLE III - MEMBERSHIP

The Friends shall comprise the original seven (7) founders, as recorded by the then Director of the Library and confirmed by the President of Amherst College, and additional persons admitted to membership as provided in the By-Laws. The Librarian of the College, the Special Collections Librarian and the Reference Librarian shall be ex-officio voting members of the Friends. Any person interested in the purposes of the Friends shall be eligible for membership.

ARTICLE IV - BY-LAWS

This Constitution shall be supplemented and implemented by By-Laws which shall provide for membership, contributions, meetings, a Council which shall be the governing body of the Friends, officers, committees, funds, amendments and such other matters as may be deemed necessary or proper from time to time. The original By-Laws shall be adopted either by a two-thirds vote of the members present at a meeting held for that purpose or by the written approval of two-thirds of the voting members at the time of adoption.

ARTICLE V - GOVERNMENT

Section 1. The government of the Friends is vested in the Council, consisting of the Librarian of the College, the Special Collections Librarian, the Reference Librarian, the Editor of the <u>Newsletter</u>, the Librarian Emeritus and fifteen (15) members to be elected by the Friends from the membership. The elected members shall be divided into three classes of five members each.

Section 2. The Council shall be comprised and shall function in accordance with the provisions of the By-Laws.

Section 3. The decision of the Council shall control and be binding on all questions of construction of the Constitution and By-Laws.

ARTICLE VI - DISSOLUTION

Section 1. Dissolution of the Friends may be effected at or as of any time (a) by a two-thirds vote of the entire voting membership (i) of the Council or (ii) of the Friends, at any regular or special meeting of either, provided that at least two (2) weeks notice is given to all authorized to vote at such meeting that dissolution is to be considered at it, or (b) by action of the Trustees of Amherst College.

Section 2. In case of dissolution any assets remaining after the payment of all obligations shall be transferred to and become part of the general funds and property of Amherst College, for the uses and purposes of the Library.

ARTICLE VII - AMENDMENTS

This Constitution may be amended at any time by the written consent or concurrent action of not less than two-thirds of the voting members present at any duly called meeting of members, the notice of which shall state in substance that an amendment of this Constitution will be proposed.

CONSTITUTION FOR

THE FRIENDS OF THE HOWARD COLMAN LIBRARY

ROCKFORD COLLEGE, ROCKFORD, ILLINOIS

ARTICLE I - NAME

    Section 1. The name of this organization shall be The Friends of the Howard Colman Library, Rockford College.

ARTICLE II - PURPOSE

    Section 1. The purpose of this organization shall be

       (a) to promote an interest in the Howard Colman Library among the alumni, the Rockford community, and the general public;

       (b) to serve as a medium through which the Friends of the Howard Colman Library may attract gifts of books, manuscripts, other appropriate library materials, bequests of money, etc., in support of the Howard Colman Library collection and programs;

       (c) to assist the Howard Colman Library and its staff by increasing the facilities and resources of the library, through exhibits, programs, publications, and other appropriate means of promoting the interests of the library.

ARTICLE III - MEMBERSHIP

    Section 1. Membership shall be open to all individuals and organizations who share in the purpose of the Friends.

    Section 2. The various types of membership, and the dues for each category, shall be determined by the Executive Committee.

ARTICLE IV - OFFICERS AND EXECUTIVE COMMITTEE

    Section 1. The officers of this organization shall consist of a Chairman, a Vice-Chairman, a recording and corresponding Secretary, and a Treasurer.

    Section 2. The Executive Committee shall consist of the officers and not less than eight nor more than twelve other members of the organization.

    Section 3. The Officers and Executive Committee shall be appointed by the Director of the Howard Colman Library, with the approval of the President of Rockford College. The Director of the Library shall be an ex-officio member of the Executive Committee, without a vote except to break a tie vote. He shall have a veto power over all decisions of the officers and Executive Committee which in his opinion are not in the best interests of the Howard Colman Library.

Section 4. The terms of office for the officers shall be for one year, and they shall be eligible for re-appointment. The terms of office for members of the Executive Committee shall be for one, two, or three years initially, with the terms of four members expiring each year. Any vacancy shall be filled by appointment of the Director of the Library, with the approval of the President of Rockford College, to finish the unexpired term. Members of the Executive Committee are eligible for re-appointment.

ARTICLE V - DUTIES OF THE OFFICERS AND THE EXECUTIVE COMMITTEE

Section 1. The Chairman of the Executive Committee shall preside at all meetings, appoint all committees, and carry out all other duties connected with the office.

Section 2. The Vice-Chairman shall assist the Chairman, and shall perform the duties of the Chairman in case of his absence.

Section 3. The recording and corresponding Secretary shall record the minutes of all meetings of the organization; shall keep a list of members and their addresses; shall notify the officers and members of the Executive Committee of the time and place of meetings; and shall provide an agenda of all regularly scheduled meetings. The Secretary shall conduct the correspondence of the Friends, and keep accurate and complete records of all correspondence.

Section 4. The Treasurer shall administer, as directed by the Executive Committee and with the approval of the Vice-President for Finance of Rockford College, all funds which comprise the restricted accounts, and submit an annual report to the Executive Committee.

Section 5. The Executive Committee shall appoint a Parliamentarian skilled in Roberts' Rules of Order. The Parliamentarian shall rule on all conflicts of procedure in meetings of the Executive Committee, and his ruling shall be binding.

Section 6. The Executive Committee shall appoint an Editor, who will serve for an indefinite term, from among the members of the Executive Committee. The Editor shall supervise any publications of newsletters and other publications authorized by the Executive Committee.

Section 7. The Executive Committee shall manage all of the affairs of the Friends, and direct the disbursement of funds.

ARTICLE VI - AMENDMENTS

Section 1. Amendments to the Constitution may be proposed at any regularly scheduled meeting, and can be voted on at that time, or tabled for consideration at the next general meeting. A two-thirds vote of the Officers and Executive Committee present is required for ratification of any amendment.

ARTICLE VII - CONSTRUCTION OF CONSTITUTION AND BY-LAWS

Section 1. All questions of interpretation of the Constitution and By-Laws shall be determined by the Officers and Executive Committee, and shall be binding upon the membership.

FRIENDS OF ABILENE CHRISTIAN UNIVERSITY LIBRARY

CONSTITUTION

ARTICLE I - NAME

The name of this organization shall be "Friends of Abilene Christian University Library."

ARTICLE II - PURPOSE

Section A. The purpose of this organization shall be to promote appreciation among the entire constituency of the University of the importance of the Library as the center of academic life of the institution. To accomplish this end the group will endeavor to promote an understanding of the Library's present resources and services, its problems, and its needs. The group will also endeavor to foster a favorable climate for the support of the resources, physical facilities, and services of the Library.

Section B. This organization shall at all times cooperate with the administration, the Librarian, and the Faculty Library Committee at the school.

ARTICLE III - MEMBERSHIP AND DUES

Section A. Any person interested in the Library and its development shall be eligible for membership.

Section B. The kinds of memberships available with their annual dues shall be: Student Membership $3.00, Regular Membership $10.00, Sustaining Membership $50.00. Dues for Life Membership shall be $200.00. Honorary Members may be elected by the directors after nomination by members of the Friends group.

Section C. The fiscal year shall begin January 1 and extend through December 31. Dues for the current year may be paid anytime after the beginning of the fiscal year. Notice of dues payable shall be sent out by the Vice President for Membership each year before the annual Lectureship dinner.

ARTICLE IV - OFFICERS

The officers shall consist of a President, a Vice President for Programs, a Vice President for Membership, a Vice President for Public Relations, a Vice President for Resources, a Treasurer, a Secretary, and approximately thirty directors, divided between the Abilene area and elsewhere. The Executive Board shall consist of the officers and two directors appointed by the President.

ARTICLE V - ELECTION OF OFFICERS

Officers shall be nominated by a committee appointed by the Executive Board, and election shall be by majority vote taken during the annual membership meeting.

ARTICLE VI - TERMS OF OFFICE

Terms of office for the President, Vice Presidents, Treasurer, and Secretary are for one year or until their successors are chosen. Terms of office shall begin immediately after election at the annual Lectureship Dinner and shall terminate the next year upon the election of a new slate of officers. Directors shall serve three-year terms. Vacancies for all offices occurring during the year may be filled by the Executive Board.

ARTICLE VII - DUTIES OF OFFICERS

Section A. The President shall preside at all meetings, appoint all standing committees, and carry on any other duties connected with the office.

Section B. The Vice Presidents for Program, Membership, Public Relations, and Resources shall perform the duties implied by their titles, cooperating with the President and the Board of Directors in achieving the purposes of the Friends group. In the absence of the President, the Vice Presidents in the order named above shall preside and perform the duties of that office.

Section C. The Treasurer shall be the custodian of the funds which shall be deposited to the account of the Friends of Abilene Christian University Library in a place designated by the Executive Board. He shall keep accurate and complete records of the funds and prepare a report on them at the annual meeting or at the request of the President. He shall also be responsible for sending notices of dues payable during May of each year.

Section D. The Secretary shall be responsible for the correct recording of the minutes, shall read the minutes of the previous meetings, shall act as Parliamentarian, and shall perform any other duties customarily associated with this office.

Section E. The Board of Directors shall meet in executive session prior to the annual meeting to conduct the general business of the organization. A full report thereon shall be rendered to the entire membership at the annual meeting. The Executive Board shall meet when called upon by the President or by a Vice President acting on the authority of the President.

ARTICLE VIII - LIABILITY

No officer, member, or committee of this organization shall make any contract or incur any indebtedness in the name of the organization without the approval of the Executive Board. Neither the Executive Board nor any officer shall have authority to incur any indebtedness beyond the amount on hand after deducting all unpaid obligations.

ARTICLE IX - DEDICATION TO ABILENE CHRISTIAN UNIVERSITY LIBRARY

This organization shall be a non-profit organization dedicated solely to the interests of the Library of Abilene Christian University. No monies or resources shall accrue to any officer, member of the board, or member of the organization. Nor shall any resources which may be donated to it be given to any other organization or any other part of the University. However, nothing in this paragraph shall preclude the expenditures of necessary funds for required organizational expenses.

ARTICLE X - MEETINGS

Section A. The annual meeting of the Friends of Abilene Christian University Library shall be held on a date set by the Executive Board.

Section B. Special meetings may be called by the President on approval of the Executive Board. Special attention shall be given to aiding the Library in providing interesting and informative meetings for the University and the Abilene community which will implement the purposes of the Friends group.

Section C. A quorum for the annual meeting shall consist of a majority of the then members of the Board of Directors.

Section D. Five members of the Executive Board shall constitute a quorum.

ARTICLE XI - AMENDMENTS

This constitution may be amended at the annual meeting of the Friends of the Library by a two-thirds vote of the members present, providing the amendment shall have approval by the Board of Directors or the Executive Board acting for it.

Approved 4/23/83

CONSTITUTION OF THE

FRIENDS OF THE LIBRARY

OF

THE UNIVERSITY OF THE SOUTH

ARTICLE I

The name of this organization shall be <u>Friends of the Library of The University of the South</u>.

ARTICLE II

The purposes of the organization shall be:

To stimulate interest in the collections and facilities of the library of The University of the South.

To provide an opportunity for those interested in this library to participate in exhibits, programs, and publications.

To attract gifts of books, manuscripts, and other materials for enrichment of the resources of the library.

ARTICLE III

Membership shall be open to any person or organization subscribing to these purposes. The classes of members and the dues to be paid by each class shall be as determined by the Board of Directors. Honorary Members may be elected by the membership upon nomination by the Board of Directors.

ARTICLE IV

There shall be a Board of Governors of nine members elected by the membership. Initially three members shall be elected for a term of one year, three members for a term of two years, and three members for a term of three years. Thereafter all members shall be elected for a term of three years excepting that a vacancy occurring during a term shall be filled only for the balance of that term. All classes of members, including Honorary Members, shall be eligible for election to the Board of Governors.

In addition to the Board of Governors so elected, the membership may from time to time elect additional persons as Honorary Members of the Board of Governors; but Honorary Members shall not vote in the proceedings of the Board.

The Board of Governors shall meet annually, at which time they shall elect a President, a Vice-President, and a Secretary to serve for one year or until their successors are elected. The Librarian shall act, ex officio, as a member of the Board. It shall be the responsibility of the Board of Governors to establish policies and plans for the organization consistent with its purposes, and to encourage and aid in the accomplishment of those purposes.

ARTICLE V

There shall be a Board of Directors consisting of five members elected by the members and who shall hold office for one year or until their successors are elected. Members of the Board of Directors need not be members of the Board of Governors, but the President of the Board of Governors shall be, ex officio, a sixth member of the Board of Directors. The Board of Directors shall elect from their number a Chairman, Vice-Chairman, and Secretary-Treasurer, and shall be responsible for conducting the affairs of this organization between the general meetings of its members. The Board of Directors shall coordinate these efforts with the operations of the Library, and the Librarian shall be, ex officio, a seventh member of this Board.

ARTICLE VI

A general meeting of the membership shall be held at least once each year, and special meetings shall be held as desired. It shall be a responsibility of the Board of Directors to arrange for these meetings.

ARTICLE VII

This constitution may be amended by vote of two-thirds of the members present at any annual meeting, or at any special meeting called for that purpose. The Board of Governors and the Board of Directors shall prepare and adopt, and may amend as necessary, the by-laws for conduct of their affairs.

CONSTITUTION AND BY-LAWS

THE FRIENDS OF THE COLORADO COLLEGE LIBRARY

ARTICLE I - NAME

The name of this organization shall be The Friends of the Colorado College Library.

ARTICLE II - PURPOSE

The purpose of The Friends of the Colorado College Library shall be to strengthen and to sustain the Colorado College Library by supporting its activities and programs; assisting in special projects; aiding in the development of the special collections; encouraging gifts and bequests, and offering opportunity for interested individuals to come together out of common interest in Colorado College and in its library, literary and cultural affairs.

ARTICLE III - MEMBERSHIP

Membership in The Friends of the Colorado College Library shall be open to all interested persons who subscribe to its purposes and objectives. The Friends, through its Board of Directors, shall have the authority to establish dues and to create certain classes of membership, including but not limited to charter membership, honorary membership and life membership.

ARTICLE IV - BOARD OF DIRECTORS

The Board of Directors shall be composed of the eight officers, five members-at-large elected from the membership, the immediate past President, the chairman of the Colorado College faculty library committee, one other member of the faculty appointed by the committee on committees, and five members of the Colorado College administrative staff, *ex officio*, to wit: The President, Treasurer, Development Officer, Director of Alumni Affairs, and the College Librarian. Elected Board members shall serve two year terms. The President, First Vice President, Third Vice President, Historian and two Members-at-Large shall be elected in the even years. The Second Vice President, Recording Secretary, Corresponding Secretary, Treasurer and three Members-at-Large shall be elected in the uneven years. Elected officers shall serve no more than 2 consecutive terms in the same office, but there shall be no limit to the number of terms a member may serve on the Board of Directors.

The duties of the elected officers shall be as follows:

President - to preside at meetings and generally to function as executive officer of the Friends.

First Vice President - to preside in the absence of the President and to serve as chairman of the Program Committee.

Second Vice President - to serve as chairman of the Special Projects Committee.

Third Vice President – to serve as chairman of the Membership Committee.

Recording Secretary – to keep the minutes and associated records of the organization.

Treasurer – to be responsible for the financial affairs of the Friends and, with the approval of the President of the Board of Directors, to authorize expenditures for the organization.

Corresponding Secretary – to conduct correspondence and related business of the organization.

Historian – to maintain an archive of the Friends and its activities as a permanent record.

ARTICLE V – RESPONSIBILITIES OF BOARD AND NOMINATING COMMITTEE

The Board of Directors shall be responsible for the general management and operation of the organization.

A nominating committee composed of three members of the Friends, appointed by the President, shall meet in February, of each year to nominate candidates for officers and members-at-large of the Board of Directors. The slate of nominees shall be presented to the general membership at the April meeting and voted upon at the May meeting. Additional nominations may be made from the floor at either the April or May meeting, provided consent of the nominee has been obtained.

The Nominating Committee shall fill, through appointment, all other vacancies that occur before the term of office is completed.

ARTICLE VI – MEETINGS OF BOARD AND MEMBERSHIP

Meetings of the Board of Directors shall be held at the President's discretion, preferably a minimum of twice each year.

A quorum shall consist of the majority of the elected Board members.

Meetings of the general membership shall be held preferably a minimum of seven times a year. The May meeting shall be designated the Annual Meeting for the purpose of electing Board members, receiving reports and conducting other necessary business.

ARTICLE VII – GIFTS AND FUNDS

The Friends of the Colorado College Library is established by authority of the President and the Board of Trustees of the Colorado College and all gifts to the Friends shall be received, held and administered as gifts to the College for the use of the Library. Gifts of cash or securities shall be deposited with the Treasurer of the College. Gifts in kind shall be held by the College Librarian under procedures generally in force concerning such gifts. However, the Friends shall have the authority to receive dues and specific gifts to be used to meet operating expenses of the organization--

such funds to be dispersed by the Treasurer of the College under proper requisition by the Treasurer of the Friends. Unrestricted gifts shall be allocated to library or related purposes by a majority vote of the Board of Directors.

ARTICLE VIII - PARLIAMENTARY AUTHORITY

Meetings of the Board of Directors and of the general membership at the Annual Meeting shall be governed by <u>Robert's Rules of Order, Newly Revised</u>.

ARTICLE IX - AMENDMENTS

The by-laws of the Friends may be amended at any meeting of the Board of Directors, after having been presented in writing two weeks in advance to all members of the Board of Directors. Such approval shall be by two-thirds vote of the members of the Board present, provided those present constitute a quorum.

ARTICLE X - DISSOLUTION

In the event of the dissolution of The Friends of the Colorado College Library, its books, records, archives and properties shall become the property of the College.

Adopted December 1, 1980.

BY-LAWS

Revised 5/5/84

FRIENDS OF THE AMHERST COLLEGE LIBRARY

BY-LAWS

ARTICLE I - OFFICE

The office of the Friends shall be located in the Amherst College Library (hereinafter called "Library"), or at such other place or places as may be designated by the Council from time to time.

ARTICLE II - MEMBERSHIP AND CONTRIBUTIONS

Section 1. Any person interested in the purposes of the Friends as set forth in the Constitution shall be eligible for membership and may become a member by making a contribution of an amount set forth in Section 2 of this Article II or by action of the Council as provided in said Section 2.

Section 2. There shall be the following classes of members:

Annual - any person contributing not less than $15 per year (or $1 per year in the case of students at Amherst College or $25 per year for family or joint membership) or an equivalent gift of books or other material acceptable to the Library. The Council may waive annual contributions in whole or in part with respect to any Annual member.

Contributing - any person contributing $25 or more per year.

Sustaining - any person contributing $50 or more per year.

Benefactor - any person contributing $100 or more per year.

Patron - any person contributing $500 or more per year.

All such members not in default shall be voting members. There shall also be a class of Life members. Life membership shall be awarded at the discretion of the Council to those who contribute $5,000 or more (in money or material or otherwise) within a three-year period, who shall be voting members and shall thereafter have no obligation to make annual contributions. In addition, voting or non-voting Honorary memberships may be awarded, but only by special action of the Council for outstanding services or extraordinary contributions to the Library.

ARTICLE III - MEMBERSHIP MEETINGS

Section 1. The annual meeting of the Friends (hereinafter called "Annual Meeting") shall be held in March or April of each year, for the election of Council members and the transaction of other business, on a date and at a time to be determined by the Council, or if not so determined by February 28 in any year then as determined by the Chairman of the Council with the approval of the

Librarian of the College. At least ten (10) days written notice of the Annual Meeting shall be given the membership.

Section 2. Special meetings of the Friends shall be called by the Secretary by direction of the Council, its Chairman or the Librarian of the College, or upon written request of twenty-five voting members other than members of the Council, specifying the object of such meeting. Notice of each special meeting shall state the time and place of meeting and the object or objects for which it is called, which may be described in general language, and shall be mailed by the Secretary to each member at least five (5) days in advance of the meeting.

Section 3. Notice of any meeting shall be deemed duly given if mailed to the person to be notified at his address as it appears on the records of the Friends. Any notice may be waived before or after the event.

Section 4. After proper notification the members present shall constitute a quorum. Notice of any adjourned meeting need only be given to Council members.

ARTICLE IV - COUNCIL

Section 1. The Council shall be comprised as set forth in Section 1 of Article V of the Constitution.

Section 2. One class of elected members of the Council shall be elected at each Annual Meeting to succeed the class whose term expires at that meeting and to serve for a term of three (3) years.

Section 3. In the case of a vacancy in the Council, the Chairman, with the concurrence of the Council or of the Librarian of the College, shall appoint a successor for the unexpired term.

Section 4. Meetings of the Council shall be held whenever called by the Chairman or Vice Chairman upon at least three (3) days notice to the other members. After proper notification to or waiver of notice by each member of the Council, its members present shall constitute a quorum. Notice of any adjourned meeting shall be sent to all Council members. Any notice may be waived before or after the event. No notice need be given of any meeting at which all members of the Council are present or of which they waive notice. The action of a majority of the Council members, present in person or by proxy at any duly held meeting or evidenced by their written approval, shall constitute the action of the Council.

Section 5. The Council shall make any other rules deemed desirable for its government.

ARTICLE V - OFFICERS

Section 1. The Chairman and Vice Chairman of the Friends shall be elected by the Council from among its members at the time of the Annual Meeting. The Librarian of the College, the Reference Librarian shall respectively, _ex officio_, be Secretary and Assistant Secretary of the Friends and the Treasurer of Amherst College shall, *ex officio*, be Treasurer of the Friends. The Editor of the Newsletter, and the Librarian Emeritus shall, *ex officio*, be members of the Council.

Section 2. Officers shall be elected severally for a term of one (1) year.

Section 3. An elected officer, with the Librarian of the College, may act on behalf of the Council whenever necessary.

Section 4. The powers and duties of the officers shall be such as are usual to their offices, or as may from time to time be authorized or prescribed by the Council.

Section 5. The Treasurer of Amherst College shall credit all funds received (a) by the College for the purposes of the Friends, or (b) which represent income received by the College, and designated to be for the benefit of, or for expenditure by, the Friends, to a special account maintained on the books of the College and called "Friends of Amherst College Library". Subject to Amherst College policy the funds so deposited shall be disbursed on the order of the Chairman of the Council or the Librarian of the College under policies established by the Council.

ARTICLE VI - COMMITTEES

Section 1. At the beginning of each new Chairman's term of office he shall, with the concurrence of the Council, appoint such standing committees as he shall deem necessary or advisable, or as the Council shall direct, including any or all of the following:

      (i)   Membership
      (ii)   Solicitation and Gifts
      (iii) Program
      (iv)   Publications and Publicity
      (v)   Acquisitions
      (vi)   Budget and Finance

Section 2. At least thirty (30) days prior to the Annual Meeting the Chairman shall, with the concurrence of the Council or of the Librarian of the College, appoint a Nominating Committee of three (3), of whom at least one member shall be from the general membership of the Friends, whose duty it shall be to confer within ten (10) days after their appointment and nominate candidates for election to the Council at the next Annual Meeting.

Section 3. The Chairman may appoint and discontinue from time to time such special, ad hoc, or task committees as he may deem desirable.

ARTICLE VII - POLICY

Section 1. The fiscal year of the Friends shall be the fiscal year of Amherst College. Funds of the Friends may be used or reserved for acquisitions for the benefit of the Library or for such other library purposes or for the future use of the Friends as the

Council may authorize, or may be accumulated for similar uses in subsequent years.

Section 2. Gifts or bequests of books, manuscripts or other tangible personal property may be accepted by the Friends for the benefit of the Library. Title to the subject matter of any such gifts or bequests shall be vested in such Library, and may be retained or disposed of in such manner, and in whole or in part, as the Librarian of the College may determine from time to time.

Section 3. All matters which might affect or be affected by Amherst College policy shall be cleared with College officials through the Librarian of the College.

ARTICLE VIII - AMENDMENTS

These By-Laws may be amended at any time by the written consent or general action, or both, of not less than two-thirds of the voting members of the Council. Any such amendment shall be effective immediately or at any later time specified in the resolution adopting the amendment, and shall be in force until the next Annual Meeting at and after which time such amendment shall only continue in force and effect if ratified at such meeting by a two-thirds vote of the membership present.

BY-LAWS FOR

THE FRIENDS OF THE HOWARD COLMAN LIBRARY

ROCKFORD COLLEGE, ROCKFORD, ILLINOIS

ARTICLE I - GOVERNMENT AND POLICY

Section 1. The Officers and Executive Committee shall make rules for its own government and policy, provided its rules and policy are in harmony with the purposes of Rockford College and the Howard Colman Library. In doubtful cases all rules and policies shall be cleared with the College administration through the Director of the Library.

ARTICLE II - COMMITTEES

Section 1. The Chairman shall appoint all standing committees and ad hoc committees, with the approval of the Executive Committee. The following committees shall be appointed at the first general meeting of the Friends.

1. Membership
2. Acquisitions
3. Special Collections
4. Memorial Books
5. Archives
6. Program
7. Publicity

ARTICLE III - RULES REGULATING FUND RAISING

Section 1. All fund-raising activities by the officers, committees, and members of the Friends of the Howard Colman Library will be conducted only with the prior knowledge and approval of the Vice-President for Development of Rockford College. All funds, including gifts and membership fees, will be accepted by the Friends only with the prior approval of the Director of the Howard Colman Library and the Vice-President for Development of Rockford College. All such collected funds, including membership fees, shall be deposited with the Vice-President for Finance of Rockford College, and placed in one of several restricted accounts earmarked for the Howard Colman Library, and disbursed by the Vice-President for Finance of Rockford College to cover the needed expenses and library programs of the Friends.

February 1978

BY-LAWS

ASHLAND COLLEGE FRIENDS OF THE LIBRARY

ARTICLE I - NAME

The name of this non-profit organization shall be Ashland College Friends of the Library.

ARTICLE II - DECLARATION OF PURPOSE

Section 1. The Ashland College Library stands over the city like a beacon, guiding pathways to individual excellence, community service, and the flowering of the human spirit. Professional competence, scholarly accomplishments and spiritual enlightenment are all nurtured here, radiating outward over the years through countless Ashland College students, alumni, and faculty into every field of human endeavor and every facet of community life: religion and philosophy, education and research, commerce and industry, marketing and banking, agriculture and labor, sports and recreation, family and home.

We, the Friends of the Ashland College Library believe that a stronger library means a healthier college community. To that end we pledge ourselves to support the Library, facilitate efforts in maintaining a balanced collection of general and specialized accessions, and encourage growth in advanced library techniques.

We also pledge ourselves to act as a bridge between the Library and the people of Ashland to the ends of making the public more aware of the Library's role and services, gaining public contributions to the Library's resources and making the Library a more integral part of community life.

Section 2. In furtherance of these objectives, the Friends of the Ashland College Library select officers and enroll members who will:

(1) Plan at least one, city-wide yearly event that will enhance the cultural life of Ashland;

(2) Be alert to opportunities for drawing upon speakers and other resources within and outside of the Ashland area;

(3) Consider ways of building up manuscript and other documentary collections through approaches to authors, government authorities, civic leaders, churches and institutional archives;

(4) Carry out the foregoing, and such other appropriate activities as may arise, with a view also of adding to the Library's non-budgeted funding;

(5) Fulfill the requirements of the By-laws of the Friends of the Ashland College Library as specified in Article V, Section 1.

(6) Undertake such other actions as will further the above-stated goals of the Friends of the Ashland College Research Library.

ARTICLE III - MEMBERSHIP

Section 1. Annual membership which shall follow the academic year (September-August) shall be open to all individuals who have interests as stated in Article II.

Section 2. Membership may be acquired by contributions to be established by the annual business meeting of the organization.

Section 3. Honorary Membership may be conferred upon persons who have made significant contributions to the Ashland College Library. This action will be determined by the Executive Board of the organization.

Section 4. Members shall be accorded all the rights and privileges normally provided which include the right to vote, hold office, receive publications and to participate in meetings.

ARTICLE IV - GENERAL ORGANIZATION

Section 1. There shall be the following elected officers of the organization: President, President-Elect, Secretary and Treasurer.

Section 2. President. The President shall be the presiding officer of business meetings and conferences, shall hold non-voting ex-officio membership on standing committees, and shall provide leadership for the attainment of the purposes of the organization.

Section 3. President-Elect. The President-Elect shall be the presiding officer in the absence of the President, shall aid the President in the executive responsibilities and shall assume the office of President should that office be vacated.

Section 4. Secretary. The Secretary shall maintain minutes of business meetings, shall assist the officers with official records of the organization and of the Executive Committee.

Section 5. Treasurer. The Treasurer shall maintain accurate membership lists, shall collect dues and other monies owed to the organization, shall maintain the organization's non-profit status, shall transact financial business upon recommendation from the Executive Committee, and shall maintain accurate financial records.

Section 6. Committees. There shall be ad hoc committees of this organization formed from time to time as the Executive Committee deems necessary.

Section 7. Executive Committee.

    a. Membership. The Executive Committee shall consist of all elected officers, the immediate past president of the organization, and all existing committee chairmen. The Committee will include at least one Ashland College student.

    b. Duties. This Executive Committee shall be the policy-making body of the organization.

Section 8. Advisory Board. An advisory board will be appointed by the Executive Committee to assist the committee in fulfilling the goals of the organization.

ARTICLE V - MEETINGS

Section 1. Annual Meeting. An annual meeting shall be held at such time and place as determined by the Executive Committee to present a year end report of finances, activities and future plans and to hold election of officers.

Section 2. Special Meetings. Special meetings of the organization shall be called by the President at the direction of the Executive Committee.

Section 3. Rules of Order. The business of the organization shall be conducted according to Roberts' Rules of Order, Newly Revised.

Section 4. Quorums. A quorum for the annual and/or special meetings of this organization shall be the members present.

ARTICLE VI - NOMINATIONS AND ELECTIONS

Section 1. The Executive Committee shall form as an Ad Hoc Nominating Committee.

Section 2. Election Procedure. All nominees identified by the Nominating Committee and nominated from the floor shall be presented in person by name at the annual business meeting.

Section 3. Assumption of Office. Each elected officer of the organization shall assume office upon conclusion of the annual business meeting at which such officer was elected.

Section 4. Duration of Office. All officers who are elected shall serve for a period of one year.

Section 5. Vacancies. In the event that any officer or executive committee member ceases to be a member of the organization, the Executive Committee shall declare a position vacant. If the vacancy occurs in the office of the President, the President-Elect shall become the President. If such vacancy occurs in any other elective office or executive committee, the Executive Committee shall fill such vacancy by appointment from the regular membership rolls. Such an appointment shall be effective only until the next annual meeting.

ARTICLE VII - AMENDMENTS TO THESE BY-LAWS

These By-Laws may be amended by the following procedure:

1. Any member may propose amendments.

2. Proposed amendments shall be submitted in writing to the Executive Committee prior to the annual meeting.

3. The Executive Committee shall distribute in writing all proposed amendments together with its recommendations for approval or rejection to members.

4. Proposed amendments to these By-Laws may be approved or further amended at the annual business meeting of the organization by means of simple majority vote of those members present and voting.

BY-LAWS

CROSBY LIBRARY ASSOCIATES

CROSBY LIBRARY, GONZAGA UNIVERSITY
SPOKANE, WASHINGTON

ARTICLE I - NAME

The name of the organization will be Crosby Library Associates.

ARTICLE II - PURPOSE

The purpose of the Crosby Library Associates shall be: to serve as a medium through which persons who share an enthusiasm for books or related materials, and the ideas they contain, may become acquainted and deepen their knowledge of such matters; to encourage an understanding and appreciation of the importance of Crosby Library and its collections; to increase the financial support of Crosby Library; and to attract gifts of books, manuscripts, and other appropriate material beyond the command of the Library's normal budget.

ARTICLE III - MEMBERSHIP

1. Persons interested in the purpose of the organization shall be eligible for membership

2. Admission to membership will be conferred by the Board of Directors upon receipt of application for membership in one of the following classes:

    a. Student Member, upon annual payment of $5.00
    b. Associate Member, upon annual payment of $10.00
    c. Patron Member, upon annual payment of $25.00 or more
    d. Donor Member, upon annual payment of $100.00 or more
    e. Benefactor Member, upon annual payment of $1000.00 or more, or upon acceptance of a donation of equivalent value by Crosby Library
    f. Life Member, upon election of the Board of Directors in recognition of outstanding contributions to the advancement of the purpose of the Associates

3. The membership year shall coincide with the fiscal year of Gonzaga University, June first through May thirty-first.

4. All members shall be eligible to attend meetings, hold elective office, and fully participate in programs or activities of the Associates. Other privileges appropriate to specific classes of membership may be established by the Board of Directors.

ARTICLE IV - MEETINGS

1. An Annual Meeting of the Crosby Library Associates shall be held each year at a time and place to be established by the Board of Directors.

2. Special Meetings may be held at such times as may be deemed necessary or desirable by the Board.

3. A notice of the Annual Meeting and any Special Meeting will be distributed to members at least ten days prior to the meeting date.

4. The members present shall constitute a quorum at any meeting.

ARTICLE V - BOARD OF DIRECTORS

1. There shall be a Board of Directors of at least nine members, one of whom shall be the Director of Crosby Library. The President of the University shall be an additional and ex officio member of the Board. Three new members of the Board shall be elected annually for terms of three years. The Board of Directors shall elect new Board members from a slate presented by a nominating committee after reviewing suggestions from the general membership.

2. The Board of Directors shall determine the policies, programs, activities, and the governing rules of the organization. At all times the Board of Directors will act in consonance with the philosophy and objectives of Gonzaga University.

3. The Board of Directors shall meet at least two times each year, at a time and place to be established by the Chairman, to transact the normal business of the Associates.

4. An Executive Committee consisting of the Officers and two Board members designated by the Board shall be empowered to act for the Board of Directors between meetings.

5. The organizers of the Crosby Library Associates shall comprise its initial Board of Directors. Upon approval of these By-Laws the Board of Directors shall, by lot, assign one-third of its members to three-year terms, one-third of its members to two-year terms, and one-third of its members to one-year terms. Upon expiration of these assigned terms, new Directors shall be elected as provided in these By-Laws.

ARTICLE VI - OFFICERS AND DUTIES

1. The Board of Directors shall elect two of its members to serve as President and Vice-President of the Crosby Library Associates for a term of one year.

2. The Director of the Crosby Library shall serve as Secretary-Treasurer.

3. The President shall preside at all meetings and appoint all committees with the aid of the Board of Directors.

4. The Vice-President shall assist the President and, in the absence of the President, shall discharge the duties and responsibilities of the President.

5. The Secretary-Treasurer shall be responsible for implementing the decisions of the organization, its Board and Committees, maintaining all appropriate records, carrying on all correspondence, making financial reports to the Board, and performing such other duties as the Board of Directors shall require.

ARTICLE VII - FUNDS AND LIABILITY

1. All funds received by the organization shall be considered to be contributions to Gonzaga University, thus fully tax-deductible, and shall be deposited in a special restricted account for the Crosby Library Associates established by the Controller of Gonzaga University.

2. All funds shall be disbursed through the Controller of Gonzaga University at the direction of the Secretary-Treasurer, with the approval by a majority of the Board of Directors.

3. No member of the organization shall be liable except for unpaid dues; and no personal liability shall in any event attach to any member of this organization in connection with any of its undertakings. All liabilities of the organization shall be limited to the common funds and assets. Neither the Board of Directors nor the Officers shall have authority to borrow money or incur indebtedness or liability in the name of or on behalf of this organization.

ARTICLE VIII - RATIFICATION AND AMENDMENTS

1. These by-laws shall take effect upon ratification by two-thirds of the members of the initial Board of Directors who shall be considered to be the official organizers of the Crosby Library Associates.

2. These by-laws may be amended by a two-thirds vote of the full Board of Directors.

BYLAWS

GUSTAVUS LIBRARY ASSOCIATES

ARTICLE I - NAME

This organization shall be known as the Gustavus Library Associates.

ARTICLE II - PURPOSE

The Gustavus Library Associates provides financial support and offers its members a way to be involved in the activities of the Folke Bernadotte Memorial Library. A program of cultural events and continuing education will be planned each year for members.

ARTICLE III - RELATIONSHIP TO GUSTAVUS ADOLPHUS COLLEGE

This organization is and shall remain a function of Gustavus Adolphus College and shall be subject to the jurisdiction of the college as part of its general development effort. Its intent shall be to supplement, not replace, the regular fund-raising program of the college.

ARTICLE IV - MEMBERS AND CONTRIBUTIONS

Section 1. Membership in this organization shall be as follows:

a. Regular Members shall be those individuals making an annual contribution to the organization. They shall be further classified by the amount of their contribution as annually established by the Board of Directors.

b. Organization and/or Corporate Memberships shall be encouraged and set up with the Board of Directors and college Office of Development.

c. Honorary Memberships may be conferred by unanimous vote of the Board of Directors upon those who have given distinguished service to the organization and/or those of distinguished position in the community. Such members shall be entitled to all the privileges of the organization except the right to hold office and to vote.

Section 2. Member Privileges. Each member shall be privileged to attend meetings, etc. of the organization as a whole or of any of its chapters.

All regular members shall be eligible to serve on the Board of Directors or any of the various committees of the organization.

Section 3. Listing, Relisting and Multiple Listing. Regular members shall be listed according to the amount of their annual contribution. (Article IV, Section A)

Regular members shall be relisted annually in accordance with the amount of their annual contribution. (Article VI, Section A)

No member shall be listed in more than one class. Each member who is eligible for listing in more than one class shall be listed in such class as the Board of Directors may determine in each case.

Section 4. Members Dropped. Any member may be dropped from membership by vote of the Board of Directors, provided, however, due notice has been given to the member prior to such action.

Section 5. Contribution Renewal. Contributions for regular membership are renewable annually.

Section 6. Records. Membership lists and contribution records shall be maintained and periodically examined. (Article VIII, Section 13A)

ARTICLE V - GENERAL MEMBERSHIP MEETINGS

No provision is herein made for any meetings of the general membership. Such meetings shall remain in the option of the President and the Board of Directors.

ARTICLE VI - BOARD OF DIRECTORS

Section 1. Members of the Board of Directors shall consist of the following persons who shall be directors by reason of their offices: The Chairman of the Board (optional), President, 1st Vice-President or President-Elect, other Vice Presidents, Secretary, Finance Officer, Standing Committee Chairman (Membership, Publicity, Remembrances for all Reasons, Volunteer and Nominating Committees), Recent Graduate Representative, Historian, Liaison to the Library, Chapter Delegates, other necessary appointees and Advisors. (Article VIII) The management of this organization and the conduct of its business shall be the responsibility of said Board of Directors.

Section 2. Quorum shall consist of 1/3 members of the Board of Directors. A majority of the directors present shall decide all questions before them.

Section 3. Qualifications and Terms of Office. All elected and appointed officers shall hold office as stated in Article IX of these bylaws. They shall serve until their successors have been elected and/or appointed. They shall be elected or appointed from the membership.

Board positions may be combined. Board members may succeed themselves.

This Board shall not be limited in number.

Section 4. Vacancies in an elective office, however caused, shall be filled by appointment by the President, with the approval of the Board, for the unexpired term. Vacancies in an appointive office shall be filled by appointment by the President.

Section 5. Meetings. Board meetings shall be held at such times and places as the Board may determine, the minimum being four meetings per year. However, the last meeting of the year must be held within 30 days of the end of the fiscal year. A part of the business of this meeting shall be the election of officers for the coming year.

Special meetings may be called by the President or upon the request of three Board members.

Section 6. Notice. All meetings shall be held on such notice, if any, as the Board may prescribe, but any business may be transacted at any meeting without mention of such business in the notice, if any, of the meeting.

Section 7. Vote. Directors may cast their vote only in person.

ARTICLE VII - EXECUTIVE COMMITTEE

Section 1. Members. The President with the approval of the Board of Directors shall appoint an Executive Committee of not less than three directors, one of whom shall be the President.

Section 2. Quorum. A majority of the Executive Committee shall constitute a quorum for the transaction of any business. In the event one or more of the Executive Committee shall be opposed to the decision of the Executive Committee, the question shall be referred to the Board of Directors who shall make the decision thereon.

Section 3. Meetings of the Executive Committee shall be held at such times and places designated by the President, or in the President's absence, by the 1st Vice President or President-Elect.

Section 4. Limitations. The Executive Committee shall not have the power to fill a vacancy in any elective office or in its own memmbership or in the Board of Directors, to call a meeting of the general membership, or to employ or discharge any Executive Director of this organization.

ARTICLE VIII - DUTIES OF OFFICERS AND DIRECTORS

Section 1. The Chairman of the Board is a position to be created, determined, and defined by the President, the Board of Directors and the person filling the position. This is an optional position.

Section 2. The President shall preside over all meetings of the membership, the Board of Directors and of the Executive Committee and have all authority ordinarily held by the president of an organization, to include serving as ex-officio member of all committees and filing of an annual report.

Section 3. The First Vice President or President-Elect shall perform such duties as the President may designate, and in the absence of the President, shall perform the duties of the President.

The First Vice President may also be the President-Elect.

Section 4. Other Vice Presidents shall fulfill responsibilities and duties as defined by the President and the Board. A Vice President may serve in more than one position on this Board, and there may be more than one Vice President at the discretion of the President.

Section 5. The Secretary shall take and distribute to the board members minutes of its meetings and perform additional duties required of the office.

Section 6. The Finance Officer coordinates financial records with the Office of Development, prepares the financial report for board meetings and performs additional duties required of the office.

Section 7. Standing Committee Chairmen shall represent the Membership, Publicity, Remembrances for all Reasons, Volunteer, and Nominating Committees. (Article X)

Section 8. The Recent Graduates Representative shall represent the graduates of the last ten years and encourage their membership and participation.

Section 9. A Liaison to the Library shall coordinate with the Board the services, events and ideas of the Folke Bernadotte Memorial Library.

Section 10. The Historian shall collect and write historical data on the organization.

Section 11. Affiliate Delegates shall represent their local organization. (Article XI, Section 4)

Section 12. Other Appointees. The President shall appoint such others as necessary to conduct the business of the organization.

Section 13. Advisory Members shall be appointed by the President. They may or may not be members of this organization. While serving in this advisory capacity, they shall have no voting power.

Advisors shall include:

a. The Executive Director who shall be responsible to the Gustavus Library Associates Board of Directors as well as to the Office of Development of the college. The duties shall include the keeping of a complete and permanent record of the proceedings of the Board of Directors, the Executive Committee, and the meetings of the general membership, if there be any. Such records shall be open for inspection by any member at any time. The Executive Director is responsible for all clerical work of the organization, issues notices of meetings, arranges for elections, prepares membership and contribution records, represents the organization wherever and whenever necessary or advisable, acts as editor of any regular or special publications issued in the name of the organization and does all things necessary to carry out the purpose of the organization.

   b. The Folke Bernadotte Memorial Library Director of Learning Resources who shall contribute guidance and counsel.

   Advisors may also include:

   a. The Past President who shall serve at the discretion of the President for the regular term immediately following the last term served in office as president.

   b. Others who may be considered necessary or advisable by the President or the Board.

   Section 14. Ad Hoc and Special Committee Chairmen shall be appointed as the need arises. (Article X, Section 2)

ARTICLE IX - ELECTION AND APPOINTMENT OF OFFICERS AND DIRECTORS

   Section 1. Election. Ninety days prior to the end of the fiscal year, the President and the Board of Directors shall appoint four persons to serve with the Nominating Committee Chairman as the Nominating Committee.

   Sixty days prior to the end of the fiscal year, this committee shall submit to the Board of Directors an official slate of officers proposed for the coming year.

   At the last regular meeting of the retiring Board of Directors, which shall be held within 30 days of the end of the fiscal year, the retiring Board shall elect the officers for the coming year.

   Elected officers and their terms of office shall be according to the following schedule:

Officers	Year Elected	Term of Office
President	Odd Numbered	2 years
1st Vice President or President-Elect	Odd Numbered	2 years
Finance Officer	Even Numbered	2 years
Secretary	Even Numbered	2 years
Standing Committee Chairmen:		
Membership	Annually	1 year
Publicity	Annually	1 year
Remembrances for All Reasons	Annually	1 year
Volunteer	Annually	1 year
Nominating	Annually	1 year

   Section 2. Appointment. At the first regular meeting of the new Board of Directors, the newly-elected President shall appoint the following officers for the coming year:

   Chairman of the Board (optional)
   Other Vice Presidents
   Recent Graduates Representative

Liaison to the Library
Historian
Affiliate Delegates (if not locally elected or
  appointed, Article XI, Section 4)
Other necessary appointees
Advisors:
  Executive Director
  Folke Bernadette Memorial Library Director of Learning
    Resources
  Past President (optional)
  Other Advisors as necessary

Ad Hoc and Special Committee Chairmen may be appointed now or as needed. (Article VIII, Section 14) (Article X, Section 2)

Section 3. Terms of Office. All elected members of the Board of Directors shall serve as stated in Section 1 of this Article and shall take office on June 1, in accordance with the fiscal year, following their election.

All appointed officers shall hold office for one year and take office immediately following their appointment.

ARTICLE X - COMMITTEES

Section 1. The Standing Committees Chairmen shall be elected (Article IX). The committee members shall be appointed by the President and each Committee Chairman.

The Standing Committees shall be:

a. Membership Committee which promotes annual membership. The membership list shall be maintained and listed by the Executive Director and shall be periodically reviewed by the Membership Committee and the Board.

b. Publicity Committee which coordinates with the News Services media releases and announcements of events and activities. Members of this committee shall aid the Historian by providing newspaper clippings and other pertinent data for the Historian's files.

c. The Remembrances for All Reasons Committee which promotes, accepts and acknowledges remembrance gifts to the Library.

d. The Volunteer Committee which supplies volunteer aid when necessary.

e. The Nominating Committee which prepares a slate of nominees for elected Board offices. (Article IX)

Section 2. Ad Hoc and Special Committee Chairmen for Special Programs, Projects, Fund raisers, etc., shall be appointed by the President and shall meet with the Board of Directors as necessary. The duties of the committee shall be outlined at the time of the appointment of the chairman.

Committee members shall be appointed by the President and each Committee Chairman.

ARTICLE XI - AFFILIATES

Section 1. Organization. Local affiliates of this organization may be established by the Board. An affiliate name should be declared and the area defined.

Section 2. Purpose. The purpose of the affiliates shall be to assist the parent organization in fulfilling its objectives and to promote membership in the organization.

Section 3. Members. All affiliate members shall be members of the parent organization. Members of the parent organization shall be eligible, but not required, to be members in their respective affiliate, if there be one.

Section 4. Officers. The organization for leadership of local affiliates is optional and somewhat dependent upon how active the affiliate wishes to be. Since communication with the Board of Directors from all areas is highly desirable a Board representative, or a contact person, shall be designated in some way by the local organization or appointed by the parent Board of Directors.

If the affiliate is to be locally active, it is strongly recommended that it be led by elected officers, or an elected or appointed Executive Committee of three or more members, at least one of whom shall be the Board representative.

Section 5. Local Meetings are at the discretion of the local members.

Section 6. Local Dues over and above the Gustavus Library Associates membership contribution, are optional and shall be determined by the local members. All affiliate members shall first be members of Gustavus Library Associates by virtue of their contribution.

Section 7. Affiliate Reports shall be given to the Board. A minimum shall be an annual report which may be prepared with the aid of the Executive Director.

ARTICLE XII - FINANCES

Section 1. The Fiscal Year of this organization shall commence on the first day of June in each year and shall end on the last day of May.

Section 2. Contributions for Membership shall be annual and shall coincide with the fiscal year. (Article IV)

Section 3. Audit. The audit of Gustavus Library Associates funds is included as part of the regular college audit. That portion of the audit pertaining to Gustavus Library Associates will be available after October 1.

ARTICLE XIII - REVIEW

At least every five years the President, with approval of the Board, shall appoint a Bylaws Committee of at least three members to review and recommend changes, if any, to the Board.

ARTICLE XIV - AMENDMENTS

These proposed Bylaws may be amended at the last Board of Directors' meeting of the year by a two-thirds vote of the members present and voting. At least thirty (30) days written notice of an amendment shall be given each member of the Board.

May 23, 1978

ASSOCIATES OF

THE SWARTHMORE COLLEGE LIBRARIES

BY-LAWS

ARTICLE I - NAME

The name of this organization shall be The Associates of The Swarthmore College Libraries. The Swarthmore College Libraries include McCabe Library (the central library); The Science Libraries (Cornell Library of Science & Engineering, and Astronomy); The Underhill Music Library; The Friends Historical Library and The Peace Collection.

ARTICLE II - PURPOSE

The purpose of this organization shall be:

a. To encourage understanding and appreciation of the work of the Swarthmore College Libraries;

b. To provide a medium through which friends of the libraries may become acquainted and share their enthusiasm for books; and

c. To attract gifts of money and, consistent with Swarthmore's collecting interest, gifts of books, manuscripts or other library materials, for the enrichment of the library resources of Swarthmore College.

ARTICLE III - MEMBERSHIP

Section 1. Membership shall be open to all individuals in sympathy with these purposes, and to representatives of organizations and clubs when such representation is desired.

Section 2. Each member shall be entitled to one vote.

Section 3. Membership is for the academic year.

Section 4. There shall be the following classes of membership: Student, Individual, Family, Patron, Benefactor and Life.

Section 5. Members are welcome to use the Library's collections in any of its branches under prevailing regulations, and to avail themselves of such services as can be provided by Library staff.

ARTICLE IV - MEETINGS

Section 1. There shall be an annual meeting for the election of officers and the transaction of other business at a time and place to be determined by the Board of Directors.

Section 2. Other meetings may be held at such times and place as may be deemed necessary or desirable.

ARTICLE V - BOARD OF DIRECTORS

Section 1. A Board of Directors comprised of at least fifteen (15) members will be elected by a majority of those present and voting at the annual meeting. Ex-officio Members: The College Librarian, The Director of Friends Historical Library, a member of the Faculty, an Undergraduate. Faculty and Undergraduate members of the Board shall be appointed by the College Librarian.

Section 2. The officers of this organization shall be a Chairman, a Vice-Chairman (who will also serve as program chairman) and a Secretary-Treasurer, who shall be the Swarthmore College Librarian or his/her designated agent. The Chairman and Vice-Chairman shall be elected annually by the Board of Directors.

ARTICLE VI - DUTIES OF OFFICERS

Section 1. The Chairman shall preside at all meetings, appoint chairmen of the Standing Committees and carry on any other duties connected with the office.

Section 2. The Vice-Chairman shall assist the Chairman, and in case of absence, shall perform the duties of Chairman. he shall be responsible for arranging the annual and other meetings.

Section 3. The Secretary-Treasurer shall:

a. Record the attendance at all meetings;

b. Keep a list of the membership and notify the members of the time and place of meetings; and

c. Collect all contributions.

Section 4. In addition to the annual meeting, the Board shall meet to conduct its affairs on such occasions and at such times as the Board itself may direct.

Section 5. The following are the Standing Committees: Program, Acquisitions, Membership, Publicity, Nominating and Publications. Other standing committees may be established with the approval of the Board of Directors.

ARTICLE VII - MEMBERSHIP CATEGORIES

Student - $2.00
Individual - $15.00
Family - $25.00
Patron - $100.00
Benefactor - $250.00
Life - $2,500.00

Life memberships may be paid over a period not to exceed five (5) years. Individuals may be invited to Honorary Membership by the

Board. Honorary Members shall have voting privileges, and shall receive all meeting notices and publications of the organization. Corporate bodies may be invited to membership.

Membership contributions are gifts to Swarthmore College. Funds gathered by the Associates will be maintained and accounted through the usual college procedures. Expenditure of funds will be made by the Library through the normal channels.

ARTICLE VIII - AMENDMENTS

Section 1. These by-laws may be amended at the annual meeting of the Association by a two-thirds vote of the members present, providing that notice of such proposed amendments shall have been mailed to all members at least ten (10) days before the said meeting.

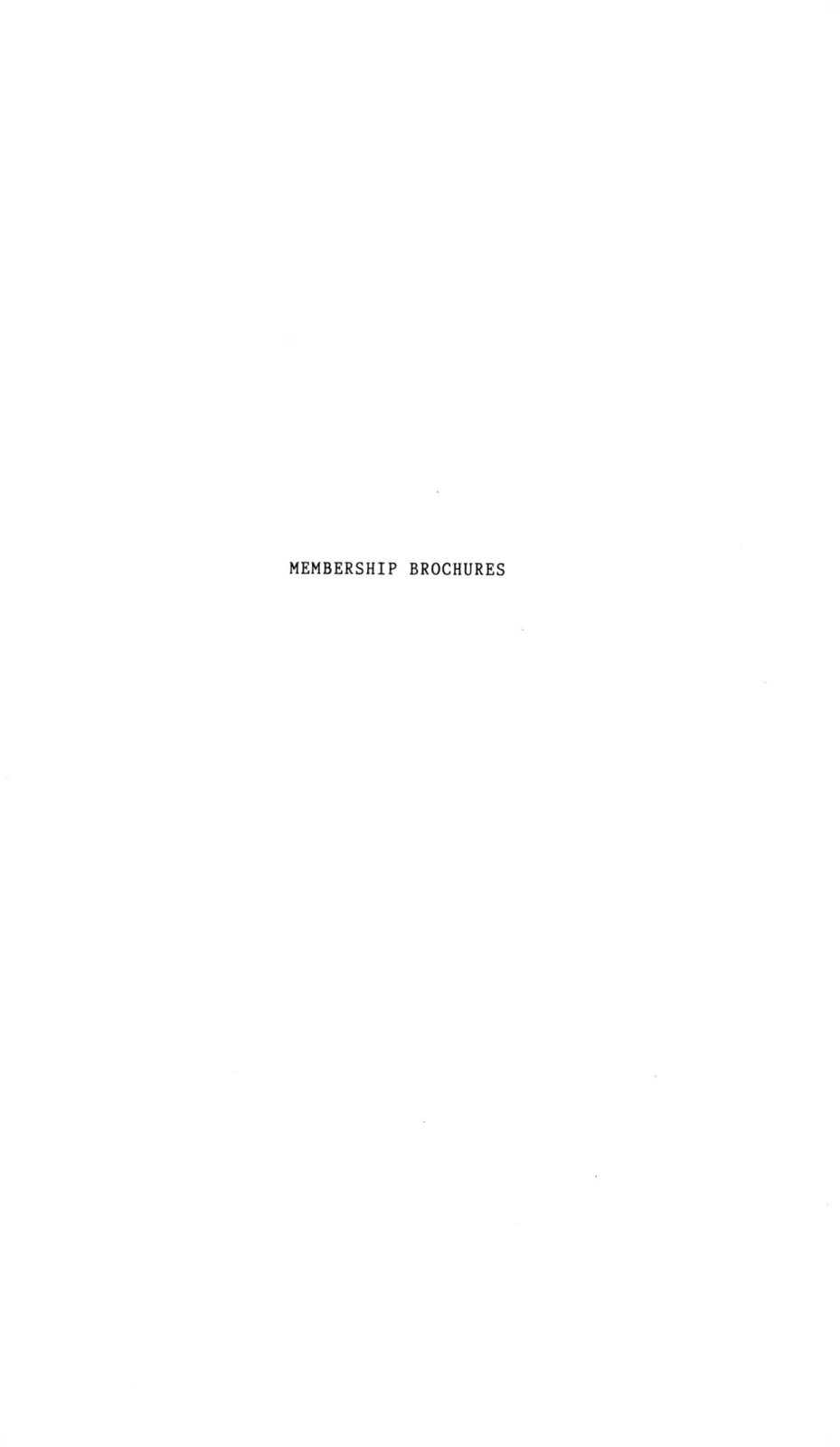

MEMBERSHIP BROCHURES

ELON COLLEGE
FRIENDS of the LIBRARY

You are cordially invited to become a **Friend of the Library of Elon College.**

The Purpose of the association is to promote the interests of the Library and to provide enrichment for its total resources and facilities.

The Privileges of membership in the association are: 1) an opportunity to participate in the enhancement of the academic life of the college, 2) a card entitling you to check out books, and 3) an opportunity to enjoy programs planned by the **Friends of the Library of Elon College** Board for the membership.

THE FRIENDS OF THE LIBRARY OF ELON COLLEGE
ELON COLLEGE, NORTH CAROLINA 27244

I/We wish to join the **Friends of the Library of Elon College** as indicated below:

Student	_____ $ 3 annually	Sustaining	_____ $ 50 annually
Contributing	_____ $15 annually	Sponsor	_____ $100 annually
Associate	_____ $25 annually	Patron	_____ $500 annually
Life	_____ $2500 or five years as Patron	Other	_____ annually

Couples may become members by contributing at the Associate level or above (minimum $25).

Student members must be 18 years old and enrolled in an institution of higher education.

Name _____ Telephone ( ) _____

Address _____

City, State, Zip _____

All contributions are tax-deductible as provided by law. Your contributions may be eligible to be matched by your employer. Please check with your corporate personnel office.

The **Friends of the Library of Elon College** welcomes gifts, memorials, and endowments. Please address inquiries about donations to the Secretary, **Friends of the Library of Elon College,** Elon College, Campus Box 2116, Elon College, North Carolina 27244-2010.

Description: The membership brochure of the Friends of the Library of Elon College is a tan card with brown print (3 1/2 x 6"). The card has text on both sides.

Friends of the
Ashland College Library

ASHLAND, OHIO 44805
419/289-4067

September, 1985

Dear Friend,

A new membership year, for the Friends of the Ashland College Library, is beginning.

I encourage you to participate in the innovative and stimulating programs planned by the Executive Committee. These include an excursion to Cleveland November 2nd, and a round-table discussion by area authors in April. Also scheduled is the upcoming fall luncheon October 12th, featuring Rick Sowash, who will present "Looking for Mr. Goodbook: How I Will Choose the 2,500 Books I Will Read the Rest of My Life."

Our contributions help insure that the library remains a dynamic resource center, housing numerous unique collections and modern online computers.

During the past year, Friends' gifts accounted for almost $3,500 in new materials--materials that could not have been purchased otherwise. Another $2,181 funded staff development, capital improvements, special printings for the library and insurance for the rarer items in the Special Books Collection.

Let us join together and show our support for and pride in this excellent facility by becoming Friends of the Ashland College Library.

Cordially,

Arthur B. Gorsuch
Membership Chairman

Friends of the Ashland College Library believe:
- that a stronger library will enhance the quality of the college community, and that support of the library will aid in assuring a balanced collection.
- that good libraries stimulate the pursuit of individual excellence, professional competence, scholarly accomplishment, and spiritual enlightenment.

Friends of the Ashland College Library receive:
- full usage privileges of the library's collections and services;
- special notices of new materials and upcoming activities on campus;
- recognition as a contributor to the improvement of the library, the college and the community, through the enrichment of available sources of information.

Printer's mark of Octavianus Scotus. Venezia (1493)

FRIENDS OF THE ASHLAND COLLEGE LIBRARY
MEMBERSHIP FORM

I (we) wish to join the *Friends of the Ashland College Library* at the following level:

☐ Pacesetter .... over $500
☐ Distinguished Member .... $100-$500
☐ Benefactor.................... $ 50
☐ Sponsor..................... $ 25

☐ Sustaining Member $15
☐ General Member $10
☐ Student Member.................. $ 2
☐ Organization or Group Membership $25

(Membership year ;uns from September through August)

Name(s) _____

Address _____

City _____ State _____ Zip _____

Please make your check payable to *Friends of the Ashland College Library* and return it and the completed form to: Development Office, Ashland College, Ashland, OH 44805. YOUR CONTRIBUTION IS TAX DEDUCTIBLE!

```
Description:  The Friends of the Ashland College Library stationery
              is off-white (11 x 8 1/2").  The membership mailing
              includes a tan reply card with black print (3 1/2 x 6
              3/8").  There is text on both sides of the reply card.
```

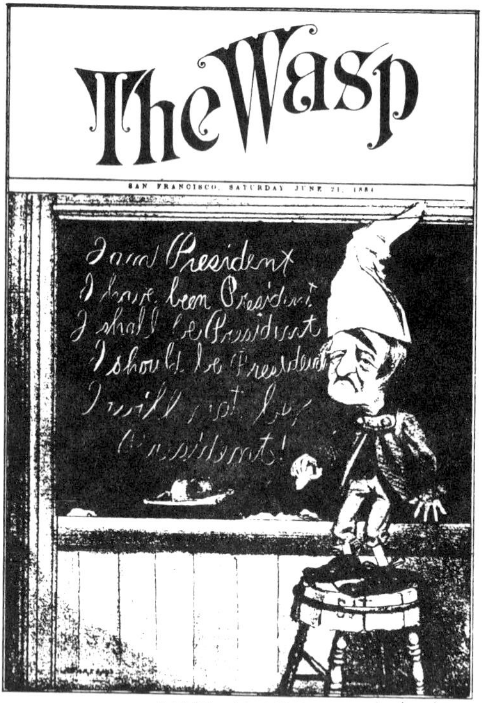

SAMMY DECLINES

ASSOCIATES OF THE
SWARTHMORE COLLEGE LIBRARIES

In the election of 1876 Samuel James Tilden (1814-1886), in spite of his having received a majority of the votes cast, was yet denied the presidency. In 1884 there was some speculation concerning his intentions as the caricature shows. Another ambition of his was more successful when, after his death, the Tilden Trust was set up to establish a free library for the City of New York. We cannot all be Tildens, but we can help provide some of the necessary support for libraries.

The Associates of the Swarthmore College Libraries—a group of book-lovers of many kinds—form a link between the campus and the community of book-lovers. Our purpose is to support the Swarthmore College Libraries, which form a resource of immeasurable value in the intellectual life of the College. The libraries need the generosity of enlightened donors. Your support will help to provide books, the purchase of which would not normally be possible from regular library funds. The Associates also provide a means whereby members can share their love of books, and at the same time participate in the further growth of the libraries. As an Associate, you will receive notifications of the varied library events that are planned. We will send announcements, invitations, catalogs, reports and occasional publications as they are issued.

If you are already a member of the Associates, we thank you for your patronage and urge you to renew your membership; if you are not, we cordially invite you to join. Membership fees are:

    Individual $15.00
    Family $25.00
    Student .... $ 5.00
    Patron $100.00
    Benefactor $250.00
    Life $2,500.00

Gifts of books and manuscripts that fit into our collections will be equally welcome upon prior consultation with the Library. Contributions are tax deductible. Your gift can be doubled if you are attached to a firm with a program for matching contributions to educational institutions.

    Beverley Bond Potter '55, *Chairperson*
    Eugene Weber, *Vice-Chairperson*
    Michael J. Durkan, *Secretary/Treasurer*

All communications should be addressed to the Secretary, Associates of the Swarthmore College Libraries, Swarthmore, PA 19081.

Description: The membership brochure of the Associates of the Swarthmore College Libraries is a one-fold, vertical white card with black print (folded 6 1/2 x 4 3/4"). The cover features an illustration from The Wasp with an acknowledgement of the Michael M. Rea Short Story Collection. The inside pages describe the Associates and indicate levels of membership.

The Library Patrons of
Occidental College

An invitation to membership.

The purposes of the Library Patrons of Occidental College, organized in 1956, are (1) to promote a personal interest in the Library's collections and their role in the academic program of the College; and (2) to encourage gifts and bequests to the Library of significant books, manuscripts, other library materials and funds for special purchases and library endowment.

Current activities include an annual dinner meeting, publication of *Occidentaliana*, a newsletter about gifts and other library news, and sponsorship of an annual Student Book Collection Contest to encourage the meaningful ownership of books by students. In addition, members have special borrowing privileges from the Library.

Developing and maintaining a scholarly library is a long-range enterprise which must have a wide base of support. In the past many worthy gifts have been received. Through membership in the Library Patrons you may share in the future excitement of helping the growth and enrichment of the Occidental College Library in addition to enjoying the association of other book lovers. Please join by returning the enclosed card.

```
                    Please enroll me as a member of the
                    Library Patrons of Occidental College

            Mr.
  Name      Mrs.
            Miss   _____


  Address   _____
            Street


            _____
            City                    State           Zip Code

  Annual membership (includes spouse)      $25
  Alumni (ten years or less)               $15
  Contributing membership                  $100 or more


  Make check payable to Library Patrons of Occidental College.
  Gifts are tax deductible.
```

Description: The membership brochure of the Library Patrons of
               Occidental College is a one-fold, horizontal, beige
               card with black print (folded 4 1/2 x 6 1/4"). The
               cover features an illustration from Rembrandt with an
               acknowledgement on the verso: Rembrandt's <u>Portrait of
               Jean Six</u> 1647. The following page describes the
               Library Patrons and the back cover is blank. A
               separate reply card (4 1/4 x 5 1/8 ") with print on
               one side is enclosed.

Everybody

Needs

Friends

Join the *Friends of the UW-Parkside Library*

Support a unique community enrichment resource

Friends of the UW-Parkside Library
C/O **the** Library Director
University of Wisconsin-Parkside
Box No. 2000
Kenosha WI 53141

Friends of the UW-Parkside Library
C/O **the** Library Director
University of Wisconsin-Parkside
Box No. 2000
Kenosha WI 53141

Thank You!

What *Friends* are for

The purposes of the *Friends of the University of Wisconsin-Parkside Library* are:

- to develop an interest in the Library of UW-Parkside
- to promote the role of the Library in education and the community
- to serve as a medium for acquisition of funds for the extension and improvement of library services and resources.

What *Friends* do

The *Friends* will support and enhance selected areas of the Library collection which are of special interest or use to the local community but which cannot be adequately supported by regular funding.

The *Friends* will sponsor programs to promote use of the Library by introducing potential users to the Library's collections and other resources.

The *Friends* will help us determine specific areas in which the local community can best augment the collection.

The *Friends* will help plan programs which will be of interest and value to the local community.

Membership in the *Friends* is open to everyone in the community.

Parkside Library Friend of the Community

UW-Parkside's Library provides a research component which complements the excellent collections of public and other libraries in the region. The Library has traditionally been available for use by any resident of the community. In fact, community users account for more than 30% of the items checked out from the Library. Regular users of the Library include researchers from local industries, history buffs, amateur genealogists, high school students, independent scholars, extension students, and other individuals working on projects requiring the use of an academic research collection.

There are a wide variety of resources available for community use in the UW-Parkside Library.

Yes, I want to be a *Friend*

__Student	$ 3.00	__Donor	$100.00
__Individual	$ 12.00	__Sponsor	$250.00
__Family	$ 18.00	__Benefactor	$500.00

Name _____
Address _____
City/Zip _____
Phone _____

__I'm interested, please send more information.

Please make checks payable to: *Friends of the UW-Parkside Library.*

Description: The membership brochure of the Friends of the
              University of Wisconsin-Parkside Library is a two-
              fold, vertical, off-white mailer with black print
              (folded 8 1/2 x 3 3/4"). The brochure includes a
              tear-off reply card.

A FRIEND INDEED

You are cordially invited to become a member of the Friends of the Eckerd College Library. The Friends is an active organization composed of individuals from all walks of life bound together by a shared recognition of the important role libraries have to play in the education of tomorrow's leaders. Through membership in the Friends, you can share in the satisfaction of supporting worthwhile projects and programs designed to enrich the educational experience of Eckerd students while enjoying the fellowship of other, like-minded individuals.

PROFILE OF ECKERD COLLEGE

With a national reputation for excellence in higher education, Eckerd College is a coeducational college of the liberal arts located on Boca Ciega Bay in St. Petersburg, Florida – 4200 54th Avenue South (Pinellas Bayway), just off U.S. 19 South and I-275.

STUDENTS 1986-87
Enrollment: 1,195
35 states and 35 foreign countries represented

FACULTY
90% have earned doctorate degree
Faculty/Student ratio of 1:14

ACADEMIC PROGRAM
Pace-setting program marked by excellence and innovation featuring over 30 majors plus individual concentrations developed around a specific interest.
Pre-professional studies in medicine, law, the ministry and education.
Emphasis on integrative, interdisciplinary, values-oriented learning.
Application of learning through internships, field experiences, study abroad programs and apprenticeships.

GRADUATES
Many have completed graduate and professional schools – Eckerd College ranks 24th nationwide as an undergraduate source of Ph.D.s
92% of pre-law students in the past 10 years who worked with our pre-law advisor were accepted by major law schools.
70% of pre-med students in the past 10 years were accepted by major professional schools; national average = 40%.

FOR MORE INFORMATION
If you have any questions, please give us a call at (813) 867-1166.

Eckerd College is related by Covenant to the Presbyterian Church (U.S.A.) and does not discriminate on the basis of sex, age, handicap, race, color or ethnic origin.

ECKERD COLLEGE

A SPECIAL INVITATION

FROM THE FRIENDS OF THE ECKERD COLLEGE LIBRARY

WHAT DO THE FRIENDS DO?

Since the infancy of the college, the contributions of the Friends have helped to enrich the library's collections and enhance the library's services. For example, the Friends recently initiated sponsorship of a rental collection of popular fiction and non-fiction books to encourage students to expand their reading beyond regular curricular demands. The Friends' generosity also enabled the library to purchase two microcomputers that are used, among other things, to produce library guides for students.

In addition to providing financial support, the Friends have also made significant contributions to the intellectual and cultural life of the college through their sponsorship or co-sponsorship of numerous events and programs, usually related to the world of books and authors.

WHY SHOULD YOU BE A FRIEND?

While the main benefit to be derived from joining the Friends is the satisfaction of helping to strengthen a crucial academic resource, there are other more tangible benefits available to members. The most direct is the privilege of borrowing books from the library's collection of over 130,000 volumes. Through the Adopt-A-Book program, you can even guarantee yourself first access to new, specially selected materials (for details see a librarian). Friends regularly receive the college's "Calendar of Events," informing them of campus activities which they are welcome to attend, and they are occasionally granted special guest status at programs for which there is normally a charge, i.e., theater productions. The camaraderie to be found at special events sponsored by the Friends is, of course, another enjoyable benefit.

HOW DO YOU JOIN THE FRIENDS?

To join the Friends just complete the attached membership application and mail it along with your check to the address given. Or, if you prefer, you can bring it in person to the library, Monday through Friday, 8:30 AM to 5:00 PM.

REGULAR membership entitles you to participate in all the Friends' activities and to borrowing privileges at the Eckerd College Library. Some specific activities may require an additional, but reasonable, fee. The FAMILY membership extends these privileges to all members of your immediate family. Those choosing to become SUSTAINING and CONTRIBUTING members will receive additional special recognition by the Board of Directors.

The membership year runs from September 1 to August 31.

BOOK-A-YEAR ENDOWMENT FUND

In an effort to develop long-term support for the Eckerd College Library, the Friends have established a book endowment fund. For a contribution of $50, a book will be purchased each year in perpetuity in the name of the donor or in memory or honor of someone the donor designates. Once an individual fund has been established, it can be added to at any time, in any amount. For example, another book will be added to the collection in the honoree's name whenever the total amount in the fund reaches a multiple of $50.

This endowment fund is an important method through which you can provide significant long term support for the Eckerd College Library while providing someone with a continuing remembrance.

To establish a book-a-year fund, please return the attached form with your check. Please designate on your check that the contribution is for the book-a-year endowment fund. It is, of course, tax deductible.

MEMBERSHIP APPLICATION

PLEASE ENROLL ME AS A MEMBER OF THE FRIENDS OF THE ECKERD COLLEGE LIBRARY IN THE CATEGORY CHECKED.

☐ REGULAR MEMBER ($20) ☐ SUSTAINING MEMBER ($50)
☐ FAMILY MEMBER ($30) ☐ CONTRIBUTING MEMBER ($100)

NAME _____ DATE _____
ADDRESS _____ PHONE _____
CITY _____ ST _____ ZIP _____

DUES AND CONTRIBUTIONS ARE DEDUCTIBLE FOR INCOME TAX PURPOSES.

MY CHECK FOR $ _____ IS ENCLOSED.

PLEASE MAKE CHECKS PAYABLE TO:
FRIENDS OF THE ECKERD COLLEGE LIBRARY
c/o ECKERD COLLEGE LIBRARY
4200 54TH AVENUE SOUTH
ST. PETERSBURG, FLORIDA 33711

BOOK-A-YEAR ENDOWMENT FUND

THE ENCLOSED CHECK FOR $ _____ IS SENT (☑ PLEASE CHECK ONE)
☐ IN MEMORY OF; ☐ IN HONOR OF; ☐ IN MY NAME

_____
(NAME OF PERSON AS YOU WANT IT TO APPEAR ON BOOKPLATE)

_____
(INTEREST AREAS OF PERSON)

PLEASE NOTIFY _____
(NAME AND ADDRESS OF PERSON YOU WISH TO KNOW OF GIFT)

DONOR _____
(NAME(S) OF DONOR(S) AS YOU WISH TO APPEAR ON BOOKPLATE)

ADDRESS _____ TELEPHONE NO. _____
CITY _____ STATE _____ ZIP CODE _____

PLEASE MAKE CHECKS PAYABLE TO: FRIENDS OF THE ECKERD COLLEGE LIBRARY
DESIGNATE ON CHECK: BOOK-A-YEAR ENDOWMENT FUND

Description: The membership brochure of the Friends of the Eckerd College Library is a two-fold, vertical, cream document with brown print (folded 9 x 4"). The brochure includes a tear-off reply section.

The Friends of
The Dickinson College Library

You are cordially invited to become or remain a Friend of the Library for 1987. Your membership will contribute to a select society of book lovers united by a common interest in history, literature, science and the prosperity of Dickinson College as a community of scholars. As a member you will receive *John and Mary's Journal*, No. 11, and enjoy borrowing and interlibrary loan privileges in the Library. You will receive a particularly warm welcome in the May Morris Room which houses the Library's Special Collections treasures, many purchased by Friends' funds.

On March 3, at 8:00 P.M. in the Weiss Center for the Arts, you are invited to attend a lecture by Leonard Baskin and the opening of an exhibit of the artist's graphic works, many of which appear in Baskin's Gehenna Press editions purchased by the Friends. On April 3 in the Holland Union Building, a membership dinner celebrating the fifteenth anniversary of the Friends of the Library will also be the occasion for announcing the winners of the international *ex libris* competition for a new library bookplate.

We note with sadness the recent deaths of two valued members: Edward A. Miller, book lover and donor of many gifts to our collection; Sara S. White, a gracious co-host through the years to the descendants of first Dickinson President Charles Nisbet, who often convened annually here. We also mourn the deaths of former members Benjamin Asbell, Nathan Asbell, Donald Flaherty and Frances Fulton.

THE COMMITTEE

Honorary Chairman: Dr. Erwin Wickert
Chairwoman: Dr. Sharon Hirsh

Dr. Neal Abraham
Ms. Katharine E. Bachman
Mrs. Eric W. Barnes
Mrs. Louise Broujos
Mrs. Hilma F. Cooper
Mr. Ronald L. Hershner
Dr. Charles A. Jarvis
Dr. Brooks Kleber
Mrs. Lois Landis

Ms. Annette M. LeClair
Mr. Ronald L. Leymeister
Mr. Mark Kimball Nichols
Mr. R. Russell Shunk
Mrs. Diane Rosenwasser Skalak
Mrs. Martha C. Slotten
Mrs. Robin Wagner-Birkner
Dr. David Watkins
Col. R. Wallace White

Friends of the Library

LIFE

Dr. Milton B. Asbell
*Yale Asbell
Dr. Whitfield J. Bell, Jr.
Dr. G. Harold Keatley
Mary Margaret Kellogg
William B. Moore
Shaw Mudge
Dr. and Mrs. James H. Soltow
Ruth Shawfield Spangler

SUSTAINING

Mrs. Eric W. Barnes
Walter E. Beach
Mrs. Harry Calcutt (Bonisteel)
+ Mr. & Mrs. Eric S. Evans
Rev. Frederick E. Maser
Mark Kimball Nichols
Boyd L. Spahr, Jr.
Robert J. Weinstein
Dr. & Mrs. Samuel W. Witwer, Sr.

DONOR

Neal B. Abraham
George and Betsy Allan
Mr. & Mrs. Frank Ayres, Jr.
Dr. and Mrs. R.G. Azizkhan
Dr. and Mrs. Samuel A. Banks
•Mr. & Mrs. G. Kenneth Bishop, Jr.
John & Ann Curley
Dr. & Mrs. Warren J. Gates
Dr. Ronald Goldberg
Dr. George Honadle
Lorence L. Kessler
Dr. Brooks Kleber
Samuel J. McCartney, Jr.
Frank E. Masland, Jr.
Mr. and Mrs. Edward A. Miller
Adam C. Mosher
Radm. Roger E. Nelson
Dr. and Mrs. I. I. Rabi
Dr. and Mrs. Wilbur M. Rabinowitz
Dr. and Mrs. Howard L. Rubendall
Allen H. Stix
Elaine M. Varner
Mr. & Mrs. Robert J. Wise

CONTRIBUTING MEMBERS

David M. Asbell
Joan Asbell
Riva Lee Asbell
Sara E. Asbell
Selma K. Asbell
John W. and Margaret W. Aungst, Jr.
Katharine E. Bachman
Sara Barakat & Michael Northridge
Charles T. Barnes
Mr. and Mrs. Robert T. Barr
Mrs. W. Edwards Beach
Gordon and Martha Bergsten
Jeffrey W. Blinn
Maj. Douglas R. Boulter
Richard N. Boulton
A. Pierce Bounds/Donna L. Williams
Dr. and Mrs. William R. Bowden
William S. Bowers
Robert J. Boyle
Mr. and Mrs. John Broujos
Carolyn Bryant
Truman Bullard
Robert and Jean Cain
Josie and Don Campbell
James and Mary Watson Carson
Dorothy Cieslicki

Mrs. Merwin Kimball Hart
Christine M. Hastings
Katherine Conway Haymes
Daniel J. Heisey
Rev. Paul Helwig
Mr. and Mrs. W. Wilson Hershner
Hon. Kevin A. Hess
LTC Frances C. H. Hickey, Ret.
Bill Hill III
The Hon. and Mrs. George E. Hoffer
Kevin Holleran
Isabel and Craig Houston
Elizabeth Aaron Hundert
Aida T. Hunter
Charles A. Jarvis
William B. Jeffries
Peter E. Kane
Charles W. Karns
Cesi Kellinger
John and Carol King
Betty and Wright Kirk
Constance W. Klages
Michael and Rebecca Kline
David and Suzanne Kranz
Lois D. Landis
Chaplain Edward G. Latch
Joanne Lavner
Robert E. Leyon
Dr. Charles H. Lippy
Howard and Frances Long
Dr. and Mrs. John Luetzelschwab
Mr. & Mrs. Thomas McKinley
Miss Jackie Martin
Elizabeth Matta Masters
Virginia (Paige) Mazzarella
Janette G. Moore
Wolfgang Müller
Kathleen L. Nailor
Cordelia M. Neitz

Mr. & Mrs. K.R. Nilsson
Andrew W. Nissly
Walter H. Ohar
Louise L. Pearson
Raymond Petrillo
Nancy J. Quadri
Virginia M. Rahal
Stevan A. Resan
Victoria Hann Reynolds
Paul C. Richards
Dr. & Mrs. H. E. Rogers
Jackie and Dieter Rollfinke
Rosalind and Kenneth Rosen
Samuel and Regina Ryesky
Patrick Sanderson
Robert D. Schwarz
Donald R. Seibert
M. Charles and Jane Myers Seller
Barry and Gerry Serviente
Mae Mountz Shultz
George Shuman, Jr.
Alan C. Smith
Deborah L. Squire
H. Michael and Cori Starry
Mr. and Mrs. C.R. Stover
Mildred Straka
Andrés Suris
Ruth Trout
Dr. and Mrs. S. Graeme Turnbull, Jr.
Margaret L. Venzke
Dr. Kenneth C. Vincett, Jr.
Stephen Weinberger
Shelly Maureen Weiss
John Wilson, (Autographs), Ltd.
Debra L. Witherow
Susan and Neil Wolf
Jeffrey S. Wood
Henry J. Young
M.A. Zengerle

IN HONOR

*Alexander Miguel Martínez-Vidal *Thomas Harlan Schutt

IN MEMORIAM

*Rev. Ira Bechtel
*Edward A. Miller
+ Dennis Klinge

•Marion V. Bell
**Charles C. & Barbara Sellers
+ + Dorothy W. Bowers

••Dorothy Warren Kepner

OUTSTANDING ACQUISITIONS 1986

The Library is grateful for a great number of unusually significant gifts from individual members this year as well as for purchases made with Friends of the Library funds. They include the following:

Two letters written by JOSEPH PRIESTLEY were purchased. A 1788 letter to Sir Charles Blagden, Secretary of the British Royal Society, describes his current chemical experiments, his need for a "stronger *burning lens*" and his desire to pursue his "more favorite study – theology." An 1801 letter written to Citizen Peregaux in Paris expresses Priestley's preference for living in France and his hopes for peace so that he can "cross the Atlantic" safely. The latter letter was added through the generous gifts of Frederick E. Maser, Mrs. W. Edwards Beach and Walter E. Beach. Rev. Maser's gift included a more complete edition than our own of Priestley's *Original Letters by the Rev. John Wesley*... (Birmingham, 1791). Walter Beach added Priestley's *Index to the Bible*, (Philadelphia, 1804). David Snyder gave us two new editions of Priestley titles already in our collection.

Student research papers have already focused on one of the Priestley letters as have editing projects with three JAMES BUCHANAN letters purchased this year. Written in 1839 and 1849 to members of his family, they represent a more personal aspect of our fifteenth president's life.

Our PRESIDENTS Collection was enriched by the gift from George Honadle of a personal congratulatory letter from Jimmy Carter.

The late Edward A. Miller was a bibliophile with a special interest in medieval art and the Library is indebted to him for his many gifts of facsimiles of illuminated manuscripts such as the *Bibliotheca Corviniana* from the Library of King Mathias Corvinus of Hungary (Hungary, 1981), and *Hortus Deliciarum* of Herrod of Landsberg (New Rochelle, N.Y., 1977).

Ronald Goldberg was the donor of a MARIANNE MOORE letter written in 1968 to a professor at St. John's University where she was awarded an honorary degree. 20 other letters written by the poet who lived in Carlisle for two decades were purchased this year. Moore's *Puss in Boots, The Sleeping Beauty and Cinderella* (MacMillan, 1963) inscribed to actress Katherine Cornell was also added.

Theater history interests were served with the addition of several letters and books by CHARLES KEAN whose illustrious family is already well represented in the THEATER Collection. Letters by other actors which enhance that collection were written by Katherine Cornell, Maurice Evans, Edwin Forrest, Mary Pickford, Ellen Terry and Eva le Galliene. Books added include Ellen Terry's *Story of my Life* (N.Y., 1909) and Thomas Campbell's *Life of Mrs. Siddons*, 2 vols. (London, 1834).

Yale Asbell and his father Milton continued the Asbell tradition of generous giving to the Library with additions to the ROYCROFT PRESS Collection, to our Judaica holdings and to the publication of *John and Mary's Journal*.

Katherine Conway Haymes, a grand-niece of MONCURE D. CONWAY contributed a family letter written by her uncle in 1907 from Paris.

Walter E. Beach's interests in political science and the Library's collections led to his purchase for us of letters by SIMON CAMERON, RICHARD RUSH, ISAAC TOUCEY, ROGER BROOKE TANEY, ANDREW GREGG CURTIN, ANNIE BESANT and H. L. MENCKEN.

From the Estate of Dr. Frances Willoughby three early English Bibles (1549, 1569 and 1599) were added to the WILLOUGHBY BIBLE Collection.

BIRD & BULL PRESS. *Roller Printed Paste Papers for Bookbinding* by Henry Morris (1975), and *Chinese Handmade Paper* by Floyd Alonzo McClure (1986).
PERISHABLE PRESS. Jacob's Dancing Tune by Conrad Hilberry (1986), and *a broad(back)side* by Walter Hamady (1985).

FRIENDS OF THE DICKINSON COLLEGE LIBRARY

I am happy to join with others in supporting
the program of the Library.

Name ....
(as you wish it to appear in our listing)

Address ....

.... Zip ....

ANNUAL MEMBERSHIP

Student	$ 5.00
Regular	10.00
Contributing	25.00
Donor	100.00
Sustaining	250.00
Life	1000.00

Checks may be drawn to the order of
DICKINSON LIBRARY, FRIENDS
Carlisle, Pennsylvania 17013
(deductible for Income Tax Purposes)

Description: The membership brochure of the Friends of the Dickinson College Library is a two-fold, six-sided, dark cream document with brown print (folded 8 7/8 x 6 1/4"). The brochure includes the current membership list of the friends group. Sample pages are included. A matching reply card (4 x 5 1/2") is enclosed.

sinu meo. ℟ Dne secun
dum actu meu noli me
condemnare: nihil dignu
in conspectu tuo egi. Ideo
deprecor maiestate tua:
vt tu deus deleas iniq
tatem mea X. Amplius
laua me dne ab iniqta
te mea & a delicto meo
munda me. vt tu deus.
Quare de Lectio nona
uulua eduxisti me:

**The Friends
of the Oberlin College Library:**
Giving the Gift of Knowledge

A Long Tradition

From the very outset, the development of Oberlin's libraries has depended on gifts from generous and concerned friends. In fact, the earliest gift bookplate—that marking a volume sent by a well-wisher in Andover, Massachusetts—is dated 1834. When William Dawes and John Keep returned from their historic fund-raising trip among the abolitionists of Great Britain in 1840, they brought back not only money but also trunks of donated books—2,000 in all, including at least one from a former prime minister—that formed the essential foundation of the College library that was to follow. For fully the first third of the College's history, more books were acquired by outright gift than by purchase.

We are careful to honor the memory of the great benefactors whose names have been associated with the College's library buildings: Spear, Carnegie, Vial, McCandless, and Mudd. But we are especially grateful for those—such as Metcalf, Holbrook, Griswold, Cook, Love, Jones, Jelliffe, Stevenson, and countless others—whose names appear on the gift plates of thousands of books used every day.

One becomes especially conscious of the tradition of donor support when one enters the library's special collections. Here, where older and highly prized treasures are kept, hardly an exhibit is begun or a student project undertaken that does not recall the generosity of some friend.

The visitor to the impressive special collections enclave on the top floor of the main library is compelled to agree. One turns, for example, to the very first volume of *The Woman's Journal*, published in 1870, and finds the gift dedication from from Lucy Stone, class of 1847, on the flyleaf, written in her own hand. One takes down volume after volume of the remarkable research collection of antislavery materials and sees again and again the name of William Goodell. And scattered among the shelves one finds gifts from the personal libraries of outstanding Oberlin teachers—Wager, Shaver, Stechow, MacLaughlin, Lewis, Artz, and Lanyi—or books given by students in appreciation of them, an honorable tradition still practiced today.

Over the years Oberlin has acquired in this way more than thirty incunabula, the first of the early printed books, including rare editions of Dante and Petrarch. The latest, according to curator Dina Schoonmaker, is a handsome 1496 Strasbourg imprint given in 1985 by Victor Obenhaus '25. For comparison, there are modern fine-press editions of William Morris and Jane Grabhorn that memorialize Oberlin's great librarian Azariah Root. There are beautiful examples of fine lithography, capped by ninety-nine gorgeous plates from the 1829 "elephant folio" of John James Audubon, most of which were purchased for Oberlin in 1926 by a group of Cleveland business and professional men. Almost as impressive is the incomparable set of photographs of Michelangelo's Sistine frescoes taken by Takashi Okamura and given to Oberlin in 1986 by Anthony O. Brown '69. There is the extensive collection of original letters and autographs of famous musicians given in 1948 by C.W. Best, class of 1890, and the original score of Igor Stravinsky's *Threni (Lamentations of Jeremiah)*, given in 1964 by the composer himself after an Oberlin residency.

In a special place of honor is an extremely rare North African Torah scroll—arguably the oldest in America—given to the library in 1912 by William E. Barton, an 1890 graduate of Oberlin's Graduate School of Theology, and restored in 1985 with the assistance of gifts from more recent friends. Nearby is a contemporary Christian manuscript, the Decretals of Gregory IX, written about 1350. This manuscript was purchased by the Relief Holbrook Endowment, a 19th-century fund that is still helping the library acquire a substantial number of volumes each year, as does a fund established by the class of 1885—a gift that is "still giving" more than a century after its donors graduated.

Some of the most useful gifts have been specialized libraries assembled by dedicated collectors. For example, Stanley Harkness '04 collected and donated to Oberlin a superb collection of books by and about the novelist Samuel Butler. Through the generosity of Yale professor George F. Mahl '41, the library has virtually every important book by or about Ernest Hemingway; many of the volumes in this collection are first editions of the novelist's early work that Mahl began collecting as a hobby. Thirty years ago, Bruce Swift '11, who assembled the unique goblet collection now owned by the Allen Memorial Art Museum, gave the library an extensive collection on Edwin Arlington Robinson, including correspondence as well as first editions. In 1964, Orrine W. June, an admirer of Oberlin with no direct connection to the College, donated a comprehensive collection of books, pamphlets, broadsides, maps, and letters concerning the War of 1812. In 1987, with the help of the Violin Society of America, the library acquired the Herbert Goodkind Collection on the making and playing of stringed instruments. This collection, which includes more than 2,000 books and auction catalogs from the 17th through the 20th centuries as well as other materials, is perhaps the most important research collection on the subject of stringed instruments in the world.

One rich cache of materials written by the explorer Ferdinand V. Hayden, class of 1850, made its way to the library many years ago by way of his classmate General Jacob D. Cox. In the spring of 1987, these materials were the subject of a major exhibit and colloquium at Oberlin to commemorate Hayden's successful effort to have the Yellowstone area he surveyed declared our first national park.

In this place, all such materials are both cherished and used. We do not, after all, seek gifts for their own sake. We seek materials that will enrich the undergraduate experience.

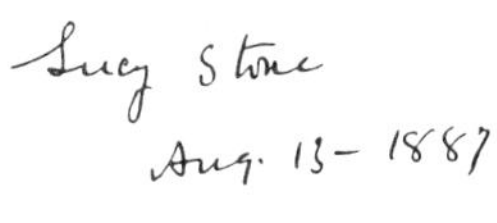

81

Gabriella Newes, a senior from Newton, Massachusetts, compares some early printed books with a Kelmscott produced by William Morris in 1892. The books are some of the sixty-five rare books on display in the exhibit "Ex Libris Frederick Binkerd Artz," a small but representative selection of the Artz bequest.

Celebrating an Exceptional Friend

On November 6, 1986, over 200 people gathered in the sculpture court of the Allen Memorial Art Museum for a symposium marking the opening of an exhibit of representative examples of the remarkable collection of maps, books, manuscripts, and prints given to the library and the museum over the years by the late Frederick B. Artz '16.

It was especially fitting that this, the first event sponsored by the Friends of the Oberlin College Library, honor Artz, one of Oberlin's most generous friends as well as one of its most distinguished scholars.

Artz began gathering the items in his three major collections in 1923, while he was a graduate student in Paris. His maps ranged from woodblock prints dating from the fifteenth century to elegantly engraved specimens of the eighteenth century. His book collection chronicled the history of the printed book roughly from 1450 to 1960; this collection included a page of the Gutenberg Bible and examples of works by all the great printers down to the Dove's Press of the early twentieth century. Later additions to this collection included medieval illuminated manuscripts and some complete Islamic and Latin Christian manuscripts dating from the ninth century. His third collection, architectural books dating from about 1500 to 1800, included some 120 volumes that now form the core of the Special Collections in the Clarence Ward Art Library.

Robert E. Neil '53, professor of history at Oberlin and a protege of Artz, delighted the audience at the symposium with an amusing and informative account of his mentor's career as a teacher-scholar. His talk was an expanded version of the memorial minute he had given to the General Faculty after Artz's death in 1983 (OAM, Autumn 1983, 79-80). Neil recalled the pride and concern Artz had taken in his rare books, gathered in the course of his many trips to Europe in the post-World-War-I era, and how much he had enjoyed discussing them with students.

Another former student, Robert M. Kingdon '49, now director of the Institute for Research in the Humanities at the University of Wisconsin, remembered his own introduction to those rare books and the pivotal influence his visits to Professor Artz's book-filled study had on his own career. He traced this influence to both his doctoral dissertation at Columbia and his subsequent studies in sixteenth-century European history. Kingdon's work has centered largely on early printed books of a type that Artz had collected, and he demonstrated by reference to his own work on Theodore Beza's *Du droit des magistrats* (1574) how a skillful researcher using such books as primary sources can contribute to the history of ideas. "It all begins with the books themselves. The debt of scholars like me extends not only to the large research libraries in which most intensive study takes place; it extends also to undergraduate

Left to right: Harold Jantz, Robert Kingdon, and Robert Neil, the principal speakers at the first Friends of the Library symposium.

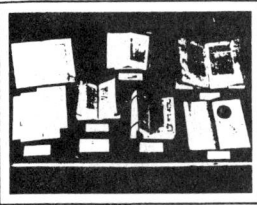

libraries like the one in Oberlin and to special collections like that donated by Freddy Artz from which our own research may draw its original inspiration."

Harold Jantz '29 and D. Litt. '60, yet another former Artz student and one whose own scholarship and book collecting was fully in his mentor's league, gave an anecdotal account of his own adventures as a scholar-collector as well as an admiring appraisal of what Artz had assembled. "It does exactly what was intended, to illustrate by concrete example the history of the book, with each of the successive stages laid out in sequence: medieval manuscripts giving way to the beginnings of typography, the master printers of Nuremburg, Venice, Oxford, and Paris, followed eventually by the best products of fine presses in our own century, with works in religion, history, geography, science, poetry, art, architecture—truly the library of a humanist! Most fortunate is the college library that has inherited such a collection, for it can present in tangible symbolic form the continuity of the human mind confronting the world in all its aspects, enabling students to see the present far better from the perspective of the past."

Connecting the Past with the Present

For me, encounters with books regularly came as a result of encounters with people. Book collecting was never an abstract matter. There was always some person pointing the way. People and books became closely intertwined, one leading to the other and back again in a way that arouses one's sense of wonder and expands one's perspective so that one has the feeling not only of having lived more widely in the present, but also of having lived in a lively past extending back through the centuries.

So it was with my first day of classes at Oberlin. Early in the morning came freshman English with Andy Bongiorno. Later came European history with Freddy Artz. What luck! And after courses increasingly came personal encounters and the chance to talk about everything under the sun. One might come to Artz's home of an evening and have him bring out a new arrival from Europe—say an elegant Aldus, in its original binding and its elegant type, beautifully surrounded by margins of just the right proportions. What a delight! How pleasant it was to hold in hand an artifact that other persons, perhaps centuries before, had also enjoyed holding in hand, one that could convey in deciphered letter form a work of the intellect, a product of the imagination, a representation of a reality alive generations earlier that still remained alive in the present for all who cared to open and read . . . .

Freddy Artz was one of the very few who exemplified the best of the art of book collecting. He, of course, derived great joy from it, but he also made sure to pass along this joy to all those who would look and listen.

—Excerpted from talk by Harold Jantz at the symposium honoring Frederick Artz, November 6, 1986

The late Frederick B. Artz relaxing in his study. Artz began his collections—which included rare maps, books, and manuscripts—in Paris during the summer of 1923, while still a graduate student at Harvard University. Students who visited his home became very familiar with these collections.

83

Erwin N. Griswold '25, former dean of the Harvard Law School, on a visit to the Oberlin library for a recent meeting of the board of trustees. He converted a valuable stamp collection into an endowed book fund in honor of his parents. Major gifts of this kind are needed to augment that part of the endowment committed to library acquisitions. The Griswold Fund supports the purchase of nearly 450 books each year in government, economics, and history.

A GIFT FROM HER FAMILY AND FRIENDS IN MEMORY OF
HELEN ESHBAUGH WARD
OBERLIN COLLEGE LIBRARY

The Need Persists

It is now more than a century since Oberlin was set on its way to developing one of the nation's finest libraries by the appointment of the redoubtable Azariah Smith Root as librarian. He started with fewer than 15,000 volumes and was soon trying to add that many every year. When he died in 1927, the collection was approaching the 300,000 mark, making it unequalled among undergraduate institutions.

Sadly, much of that collection—printed as it was on acidic paper—is now deteriorating. A prodigious effort is required to preserve the older materials for active use. At the same time, it is increasingly more costly to keep the collection up to date. Rising costs for scholarly journals continually frustrate our attempts to meet the needs of new programs, such as those in neuroscience and Latin American studies, as well as in established fields such as physics and art history.

Moreover, another basic operational cost exists today, one that could scarcely have been anticipated in the early years of the library. In those years, neatly typed cards were virtually all that was necessary for a catalog, and a resourceful reference librarian could retrieve in a nearby volume the answer to almost any question. The advent of electronic database searching and the dramatic advantages of an online computer, however, have created new demands among the users of Oberlin's library. The library must keep pace with this current technology if it is to meet faculty and student research needs.

Although some generous grants from foundations—particularly one from the Pew Memorial Trust—are meeting most of the costs of new computer systems, the expense of converting Azariah Root's cards to a modern online catalog tends to squeeze out support for other programs. It is extremely difficult to find funding for extending our special collections or for supporting the exhibits and seminars needed to make materials from those collections a vital part of our students' educational experience.

It is clear that now, more than ever, the Oberlin College Library needs friends.

—*William A. Moffett,
Director of Libraries*

These students attended a recent seminar in special collections. The library needs support for major exhibits and guest speakers who can help Oberlin comply with the recent Carnegie Foundation injunction to undergraduate colleges to "sustain the culture of the book."

A student worker repairing books in the library's mending laboratory. The preservation program, begun in recent years as a result of a timely gift from a member of the class of 1949, enabled the library to begin outfitting a modern treatment center where student workers are taught repair and elementary binding techniques. The program, which has already extended the life of many thousands of books, needs further support for microfilming and deacidification.

Oberlin College LIBRARY

THE WILLIAM EDWARDS STEVENSON
AND
ELEANOR BUMSTEAD STEVENSON FUND,
established 1957

Who are the Friends of the Oberlin College Library?

A Friend is anyone who joins in the effort to champion the role of the library in collecting and preserving books, sound recordings, and archival materials in the interests of teaching, scholarship, and personal study, or who helps us celebrate and encourage those who have contributed tangible support to the work of the library.

What does it take to join?

Simply let us know that you're interested. There are no dues.

What can Friends do?

Friends can assist the library with monetary gifts to designated book funds or gifts that augment that part of the endowment restricted to library support, by underwriting the preservation program, or by donating books or other materials. Other options include helping to attract new donors, assisting in the articulation of the history and art of the book, and helping us meet our postage and publication costs. Remember that gifts are still tax deductible if you itemize.

Are there special events for Friends?

Yes. We sponsor exhibits, auctions, symposia, and social occasions, both in Oberlin and, occasionally, in other places. We also produce special publications.

Who governs the organization?

An independent board of governors provides oversight according to bylaws developed in 1987.

FRIENDS OF THE OBERLIN COLLEGE LIBRARY
Oberlin, Ohio 44074

Students examine Oberlin's 14th-century Torah, one of the oldest-known such hand-lettered leather scrolls of the five books of Moses in the United States and the oldest complete manuscript in Oberlin's library. The restoration of this Torah, donated to Oberlin in 1912, was underwritten by gifts from alumni and friends of the College and the Premier Industrial Philanthropic Fund of the Jewish Community Federation of Cleveland.

FOR WHOM THE BELL TOLLS
Scribners
THE WAY OF ALL FLESH
THE CHOIR INVISIBLE
JAMES LANE ALLEN
ORLEY FARM
WILSON
NORTH AMERICAN INDIANS
PRIESTLEY. HISTORY OF ELECTRICITY
GEOLOGY OF SOUTH CAROLINA
WARD'S MEXICO IN 1827 VOL. I
WARD'S MEXICO IN 1827 VOL. II

Description: The Friends of the Oberlin College Library membership brochure (11 x 8 1/2") features a light blue front cover of an illuminated manuscript and a color photo of shelves of rare books on the back cover. The 8-page brochure has inside pages that are cream-colored with brown-tone photographs. A limited number of the actual brochures are available upon request from the Oberlin College Library.

PROGRAM IDEAS

President James L. Powell

and

The Friends of Shadek-Fackenthal Library

request the pleasure of your company

at a tea

in honor of Franklin and Marshall College Authors

Thursday, the ninth of April

Nineteen hundred eighty-seven

at four o'clock in the afternoon

120 North School Lane

Lancaster, Pennsylvania

[ ] *I/we will attend the Tea,*
     Thursday, April 9, 1987, at the
     President's Home
     120 North School Lane
     Lancaster, Pennsylvania

[ ] *I/we cannot attend.*

_____
Name(s)

The favor of a reply is requested by April 1st.

Description: The Friends of Shadek-Fackenthal Library hosted a tea for college authors. The invitation was printed on the front of a one-fold, vertical, cream card with a green border, using black print (folded 7 x 5 1/8") and mailed in an envelope with a printed return address. A matching reply card (4 1/4 x 5 1/2") was enclosed with a pre-printed return envelope.

NOW
15¢
BLACK MASK
GOLDFISH
RAYMOND CHANDLER
KENNEDY
FLASHGUN CASEY—George Harmon Coxe
JERRY TRACY—Theodore A. Tinsley

Associates of The Swarthmore College Libraries

present a talk by

KENNETH TURAN '67

Giving Murder Back to the People
Who Are Really Good at It:
The Romance of Hard-Boiled Fiction

Thursday, October 24, 1985 at 8:00 p.m.

Kirby Lecture Hall (Martin 201)

Swarthmore College

Description: The Associates of the Swarthmore College Libraries hosted a lecture on detective fiction. The announcement is a one-fold, vertical, off-white card (folded 6 1/4 x 4") with black print. The cover is illustrated and the acknowledgement for the illustration is on the verso: "Black Mask (June 1936) From the Collection of Kenneth Turan '67." The invitation to the lecture is on the following page. The back cover is blank.

THE PHEASANT.

(*Phasianus Colchicus*, Linn.—*Faisan vulgaire*, Temm.)

Exhibitions

Audubon Room: The Birds of Ireland: Accounts and Images, 1740-1860.

Trumbull Room: The Confederacy: From Hope to Despair.

THE WATKINSON LIBRARY
          TRINITY COLLEGE LIBRARY ASSOCIATES
                         and
            THE DEPARTMENT OF FINE ARTS
                  TRINITY COLLEGE

                Cordially Invite You To An

                        OPEN HOUSE

                With An Illustrated Talk By

                      MARTYN ANGLESEA

            "RICHARD DUNSCOMBE PARKER (1805-1881)
                    THE AUDUBON OF IRELAND"

                      Watkinson Library
                    Trinity College Library

                        March 11, 1987

                          4:30 p.m.

                     RECEPTION FOLLOWING

Description: The Trinity College Library Associates co-
              sponsored a talk on Martyn Anglesea. The
              announcement is printed in black on a one-fold,
              vertical, bright green card (folded 8 1/2 x
              5 1/2"). The cover has an illustration of a
              pheasant, the verso notes several exhibitions,
              and the following page holds the invitation to
              the lecture. The back cover is blank.

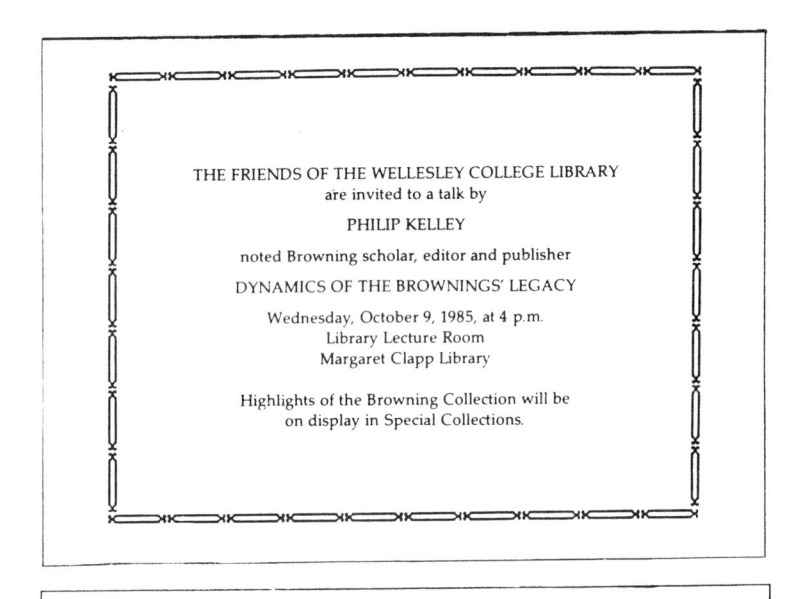

THE FRIENDS OF THE WELLESLEY COLLEGE LIBRARY
are invited to a talk by

PHILIP KELLEY

noted Browning scholar, editor and publisher

DYNAMICS OF THE BROWNINGS' LEGACY

Wednesday, October 9, 1985, at 4 p.m.
Library Lecture Room
Margaret Clapp Library

Highlights of the Browning Collection will be
on display in Special Collections.

FUTURE EVENTS FOR THE FRIENDS OF THE LIBRARY

September - October
"Ezra Pound 1885-1972 • A Centennial Exhibition"
Main cases, Margaret Clapp Library

Wednesday, October 30, 4 p.m. Special Collections
"Ezra Pound's Brilliant Appreciation of Henry James"
A talk by Arthur Gold, William R. Kenan Professor of English

September - December
"Women and the Printing Press"
An exhibition at Special Collections, Margaret Clapp Library

November - December
"From Bustles to Blue Jeans"
An exhibition of photographs from the Wellesley College
Archives illustrating changes in women's fashions from the opening
of the college to the present.
Main cases, Margaret Clapp Library

Description: The Friends of the Wellesley College Library hosted a talk by Philip Kelley. The announcement is a one-fold, horizontal, cream-colored card with blue print (folded 4 1/2 x 6 1/8"). The invitation to the lecture is on the cover with future events included inside the card.

1983-84 PROGRAM

FRIENDS OF THE

CONNECTICUT

COLLEGE

LIBRARY

Having been established in 1945, our Friends of the Library organization is one of the oldest of its kind in Connecticut. But, nourished by the enthusiasm of its members, in some ways it seems younger than ever. If anything, the intellectual spirit inherent from the beginning blossoms today with increased vitality. We wear our years lightly.

On second thought, age—youth or maturity—has really nothing to do with the Friends. What matters is sharing with one another the pleasure that comes from books. In *The Education of Henry Adams* the author wrote, "What one knows is, in youth, of little moment; they know enough who know how to learn." Borrowing the sentiment, we arrived at the theme for the 1983-84 program described in this leaflet: "How to. . . ."

Come! We know you'll enjoy the wide range of activities. Guests are cordially invited, as are new members. An extra membership card is enclosed if you would like to sponsor a friend or acquaintance.

Helen H. Johnson
Chairman

Thursday, Sept. 29, 4:15 p.m.   The George Haines Room of the Library

How to Judge a Library   *Brian Rogers, College Librarian*
The character of a college library reflects the interests and tastes of faculty, librarians, students and friends. An illustrated talk about some of the rarities and ornaments of Connecticut College's special collections.

Saturday—Monday, Oct. 8-10   Palmer Library

How to Enlarge Your Library   *Mrs. Oakes Ames, Book Sale Chairman*
The Seventh Annual Connecticut College *Book Sale*. The latest edition of this legendary event, the proceeds of which are used by the library to acquire new books. Hours: Saturday, 9:00 a.m.—5:00 p.m.; Sunday, 1:00 p.m.—5:00 p.m.; Monday (half-price day) 10:00 a.m.—5:00 p.m.

Thursday, Nov. 17, 4:15 p.m.   The George Haines Room of the Library

How to Write a Book   *Professor Cynthia H. Enloe '60*
A lecture by a prolific, successful author with much experience in negotiation with publishers on everything from cover to content. Among her books are *Politics of Pollution in a Comparative Perspective: Ecology and Power in Four Nations* (1975), *Diversity and Development in Southeast Asia: The Coming Decade* (1977), and *Ethnic Soldiers: State Security in Divided Societies* (1980). A new book is soon to be published. Ms. Enloe teaches at Clark University.

Saturday, Mar. 24   The Haines and Palmer Rooms of the Library

How to Collect Books for Pleasure and Profit
10:00 a.m.—12:30 p.m.   Individual appraisal consultations with Mr. Wyman Parker and Mr. Barry Scott, professional appraisers of literary property, repeating a successful program held last March. Up to six books may be brought for discussion and evaluation.

12:30 p.m.—1:30 p.m.   Indoor Picnic in the Library Staff Room, provided by the Library.

1:45 p.m.—2:30 p.m.   (Speaker on a bibliophilic subject to be announced)

Come for one, two, or all three parts of this informal occasion.

→

Thursday, Apr. 26, 4:30 p.m.   The Lyman Allyn Museum Auditorium

"Some Ingenious Gentleman:" How to Find an Architect in Colonial America   *Professor George B. Tatum*
An illustrated lecture by George B. Tatum, H. Rodney Sharp Professor of Architectural History at the University of Delaware. Professor Tatum teaches from time to time at Columbia University's Graduate School of Architecture and Planning and is the author of *Penn's Great Town: 250 Years of Philadelphia Architecture*, *Philadelphia Georgian: The City House of Samuel Powel*. He contributed to the well-known *The Arts in America: The Colonial Period*, published in 1966 by Charles Scribner's Sons.

As a Friend of the Connecticut College Library you may:

— borrow books

— receive assistance from the reference librarians

— enjoy any of the 1600 currently-received newspapers and periodicals (in English, French, Chinese, Russian, Spanish, Italian and German)

— and, best of all perhaps, meet with other bibliophiles

You will receive the *Library Bulletin*, the occasional *Newsletter*, and the satisfaction of making possible the continual enrichment of the special collections of fine printing, rare editions, and other unusual items which give distinction to a library and enhance its reputation.

Do you know about our memorial and commemorative book program?

For $25 or more you may ask the College Librarian to acquire one or more books or sound recordings in honor of a friend's achievement, to mark the birth of a child, to celebrate an anniversary or other occasion, or to pay tribute to the memory and life of a person loved or admired. Subject possibilities are as broad as the needs of the library, from the arts and humanities to the social and natural sciences; from computers to dance to law.

Description: The Friends of the Connecticut College Library prepared a brochure announcing the events planned for the coming year. The brochure is a one-fold, vertical, white card with black print (folded 8 1/2 x 5 1/2"). The cover is illustrated with an etching. The inside pages describe the friends group and list the events of the year. The back cover continues the events list and outlines the benefits of membership.

NEWSLETTERS

Jessie Ball duPont Library

Friends of the Library
The University of the South

Newsletter No. 8   Spring, 1987

SPRING MEETING. In view of controversies over content of school books in Hawkins County and in Alabama, it seems only fitting that the next speaker for the Friends of the Library should choose "Booby Traps for Textbook Authors" as the topic for his talk to be given on Saturday, May 2, at 4 P.M. in the Bishop's Common Lounge. Kenneth S. Cooper, Emeritus Professor of History at George Peabody College for Teachers of Vanderbilt University and the author of many textbooks, has chosen this timely subject. We have not had the pleasure of meeting Dr. Cooper at this juncture, but we gather that evolution is only one of the thorny problems in the life of a textbook author. In addition, Dr. Cooper has had a long career as a teacher, being named Outstanding Teacher by student vote a number of times before the merger of Peabody with Vanderbilt made his position redundant. The titles of some of his writings indicate a sense of humor which must have further endeared him to his students, i.e. "Did You Ever Think of Aristotle as a College Freshman?" and "Is Mitford's History That Good?" He has also written numerous articles for learned journals. Since 1976 he has published People in the Eastern Hemisphere, The World and Its People: Europe, Africa, Asia, and Australia, Learning about Tennessee, and A World View. His volume on The Mind of John Overton, Andrew Jackson's closest friend and Tennessee's most prominent land lawyer in the late 18th and early 19th century, is scheduled for May publication.

A native of Kansas, Dr. Cooper received his B.A. from Emporia College, Kansas, his Master's from the University of Nebraska, and his Ph.D. from the University of Missouri. He was a member of the faculty at Peabody from 1947 until 1980, retiring as chairman of the social studies faculty. Librarian David Kearley, who knew him as an habitué of the University Libraries, tells us that he never taught the same course twice. His talk promises to be both contemporary and delightful.

The public is cordially invited to attend, free of charge.

****

WINDS OF CHANGE. After eighteen years' service to the Library of the School of Theology, first in St. Luke's Hall and then duPont, Grace Harvey has retired from her duties as Assistant and right arm to librarian Edward Camp. Her presence on duPont's third floor is already sorely missed, but we imagine that her sunny disposition is a great boon in her full-time retirement project, the care and feeding of a five-year-old grandson. We wish her well.

****

PROJECTS GALORE. The Friends have been enjoying a buying spree since last we communicated. Would you believe that duPont boasted 460 films on videotapes when last we checked?! Not all of these were ordered from the Friends' budget, but recent purchases included big-ticket items like "Music in Time, Today and Tomorrow," tapes from a series covering various eras in music history, and three Shakespeare plays, Henry V, Julius Caesar, and Winter's Tale. To keep up to date with this proliferation you need to check the loose leaf notebook at the circulation desk.

A number of large print books have come into the library, and there is already enthusiastic response to the offerings, which include, among others, works by G.K. Chesterton, Isak Dinesen, Umberto Eco, Alice Walker, Graham Greene, John O'Hara, Eudora Welty, Charles Dickens, Charlotte Bronte, and Nathaniel Hawthorne, as well as biographies of a number of noteworthy individuals.

****

"THE OLD FOREST." Those who missed Steven Ross' film presentation of Peter Taylor's "The Old Forest" in November will now have a second opportunity to see it, at their convenience. The Friends of the Library is now in possession of a videotape of the film, thanks to a generous contribution from Isabelle P. Howe. Mrs. Howe kindly evaluated the November program for the Tennessee Humanities Council which had sponsored Mr. Ross, received an unexpected gratuity and, well, thought it only fittin'...!

****

GIFTS. An impressive new list of books has been given to duPont Library by Dr. and Mrs. Thomas F. Paine, Jr. It includes a number of works by Charles Darwin collected by the Nashville physician and bibliophile who died in January. Among them is an 1859 first edition of On the Origin of Species by Means of Natural Selection or the Preservation of Favoured Races in the Struggle for Life (did you know that was the complete title?), but there are also fine editions of Aristotle (1571), Bede (1723), John Milton (1739), Edmund Spenser (1758), and Laurence Sterne (1865), as well as more recent writings. The collection has been evaluated at $5,182, the Origin of Species, alone, at $3,500.

Dr. Paine, who graduated from Vanderbilt University and Vanderbilt Medical School, had a long acquaintance with the University of the South, having spent summers during his youth at Monteagle Assembly. Following graduation from medical school, he did an internship in Rochester, N.Y., served in the Armed Services, and then taught at the Medical School of the University of Alabama in Birmingham. He later became a member of the medical faculty at Vanderbilt. One of the couple's sons graduated from Sewanee, and Dr. and Mrs. Paine had just completed construction of a home in Sewanee at the time of his death.

NEW STAFF. Two new librarians have been added to the duPont staff in recent months. Pamela J. Ross is firmly in place as head of circulation and as a reference librarian. Mrs. Ross is a June '86 graduate of the University of Michigan, where she received her Master of Library Science degree. She holds an undergraduate degree from American University in Washington, D.C. Prior to coming to Sewanee she had served as head of circulation at Adrian College in Michigan.

Elizabeth M. ("Betsy") Grant, technical services librarian, joined the staff in mid-summer, coming from Xavier University, New Orleans, where she had been a cataloger. She holds a Bachelor of Music Education degree from Memphis State University and an M.L.S. from North Texas State.

Don Haymes is the latest newcomer, having taken up Grace Harvey's duties as Assistant to librarian Edward Camp in the School of Theology Library on April 1. He has come to Sewanee from Macon, Georgia, where he was editor-in-chief of the Mercer University Press. Mr. Haymes is a graduate of Southwestern (now Rhodes) in Memphis and holds an M.L.S. degree from the University of Tennessee at Knoxville. He also received a Master's degree in theological studies from Harvard University.

****

ELECTIONS. Rotating off the Board of Governors of the Friends of the Library at the spring meeting will be Thaddeus Lockard, Porter Ware, and Franklin Gilliam. The Board of Directors will lose Scott Bates, Sue Armentrout, and Deric Beil. Names of suggested replacements for these worthies will be presented to the membership by the Nominating Committee at the May meeting.

****

HURRY UP, PLEASE, IT'S TIME. Yes, it's time to renew your membership in The Friends of the Library for another year. We aren't going to bombard you like National Public Radio or WPLN, Channel 8, but, like them, we have a lot of good selling points. duPont Library is not a public library in the strictest sense, but it takes its public responsibility seriously, and its benefits to the community are considerable: Browsing room, music listening room, reading room, open stacks, and videotapes, all for free, not to mention the overworked copying machines which are priced minimally. Take one example: There has been an extraordinary explosion in the use of videotapes, nothing short of phenomenal, and more will be purchased as monies become available. Before you settle down for an evening with your new VCR, why not do yourself - and us - a favor and become a Friend of the Library? Everyone likes to be appreciated!

****

FRIENDS VIDEOCASSETTE TRIVIAL PURSUIT GAME. See how many of the following film facts you know. Check yourself for answers on the last page: They are all from films available at the duPont Library.
1. What Tony Richardson romp opened with Squire Allworthy returning home to find a babe in his bed?
2. What movie marked Julie Andrews' film debut?
3. What film featured the cackled line: "Well, my little pretty, I can cause accidents, too"?
4. What film featured Marlene Dietrich uttering the unforgettable words: "They call me Lola"?

If you would like to join THE FRIENDS OF THE LIBRARY, The University of the South, please fill in and mail the form below to: The Friends of the Library, The University of the South, Sewanee, Tennessee 37375-4005.

NAME_____

ADDRESS_____

TELEPHONE (Area Code)_____ (Number_____

Please indicate your field(s) of interest in library development and book collection

_____
_____

Check class of membership desired:
　　　　　　　　　　　　　　　　　____Student $5.00　　　　____Family $25.00

　　　　　　　　　　　　　　　　　____Single person $15　　____Patron $50 & up

ANSWERS: 1) <u>Tom Jones</u>, 2) <u>Mary Poppins</u>, 3) <u>The Wizard of Oz</u>, 4) <u>The Blue Angel</u>, 5) <u>To Have and Have Not</u>, 6) <u>Dumbo</u>, 7) <u>Blow-up</u>, 8) <u>Breaking Away</u>, 9) <u>The Deer Hunter</u>, 10) <u>Psycho</u>

5. What film featured the line: "You know how to whistle, don't you, Steve?"
6. Whom did Timothy Q. Mouse befriend, counsel and manage?
7. What was Antonioni's first film in English?
8. What sporty 1979 film featured the line: "No, you're not a cutter--I'm a cutter"?
9. What Michael Cimino film opened and ended in Clairton, Pennsylvania?
10. What film featured a sheriff inquiring: "If the woman up there is Mrs. Bates, who's that woman buried in Greenlawn Cemetery"?

What are my books? My friends, my loves.
My church, my tavern, and my only wealth;
My garden, yea, my flowers, my bees, my doves,
My only doctor, and my only health
　　　　　　　　　　　　　-Richard Le Gallienne, "My Books."

Newsletter of The Friends of the Library
The University of the South
Sewanee, TN 37375-4005

The Friends of the
Union College
Library

Newsletter

Schaffer Library

Schenectady, New York 12308

ANNUAL MEETING
The 1987 annual meeting of the Friends will be held Friday, March 20, at 8 pm in the Music Room of Schaffer Library. The speaker will be George Wise, historian of the General Electric Company. Mr. Wise gives a most entertaining talk, and I urge you to attend even if you don't yet know you are interested in the subject.

In conjunction with his talk, the Library will be mounting an exhibition drawn from the Schenectady Archives of Science and Technology. Ellen Fladger's article about that special collection appears later in this newsletter.

FRANCES MILLER
Those of you who knew her will join us in mourning the death last June of Frances Miller, formerly Archivist at Schaffer Library.

Frances came to the Library on a temporary basis in 1964, to catalogue some Charles Steinmetz papers. Her late husband, historian John Anderson Miller, had been one of Steinmetz' biographers. Recognizing her worth, and unconcerned with her lack of a library science degree, Librarian Edwin Tolan found ways to keep her on the payroll.

Eventually Frances became the first person to have the Archives and Special Collections as her sole responsibility. Before her retirement in 1979, her accurate, intelligent work had aided many researchers and had carried those collections a long way toward a status commensurate with their real importance.

Frances had a hand in several Friends publications, and was the author of the most ambitious of them, the *Catalogue of the William James Stillman collection* (1974).

She was a shy, quiet woman; getting to know her was a succession of pleasant surprises which has ended too soon.

THE UNION COLLECTION
Some of you may know that I was at one time Bibliographer at Schaffer Library. It has been noticed that subsequent Bibliographers have been progressively shorter and more alert, but it has also been pointed out that only the opposite development would have been remarkable.

Perhaps to show just how much progress has been made, Ann has invited me to see if I could think of anything to say about recent acquisitions in the Union Collection.

The Union Collection, the largest of the library's Special Collections, contains books relating to Union and books written by persons affiliated with Union - faculty, alumni, and others. Thanks to the assiduity of generations of librarians, and to the generosity of the Class of 1906 in endowing the Union Collection, it is an excellent collection.

Since Union's faculty and alumni have, over 192 years, written books on just about everything, the collection is wonderfully diverse, and adding to it is a constant adventure. Poetry, an auto repair manual, real estate law, a monograph on Karl Marx, a travel guide, a novel - that cross section happens to be confined to books written by people who were my friends when I was an undergraduate.

In a collection so large and diverse, many themes can be found.

It Was All Her Fault
One could document, for instance, the theme of "man as alleged victim in the war between the sexes", starting perhaps with the *Memoirs* (1824) of the Rev. Ammi Rogers, a trustee of Union from its founding until 1805. Later, in Connecticut, Rogers served a two year prison term for seducing a young woman and procuring an abortion. He spent the rest of his life peddling his mendacious book, which claimed it was all a frame-up. The Library has five of the eleven editions published between 1824 and 1846, but the first edition continues to elude capture.

The theme is continued in *My Courtship and its Consequences* (1855) by Henry Wikoff (Class of 1832), in which Wikoff chronicles his European courtship of an American heiress.

The lady kept changing her mind, once on the day before the wedding, and Wikoff finally resorted to what the DAB calls "a friendly abduction" - which got him fifteen months in the Genoa slammer. He told the story again in *Adventures of a roving diplomatist* (1857), and one would not be surprised if he also buttonholed some wedding guests.

Finally (one hopes), *Strange Sisters* (1973), by "Peter Stanley", a pseudonymous member of the Class of 1962, is an "adult" novel about a young man held prisoner (in chains) by two very imaginative sisters. The library doesn't yet own it, but it does exist, and if you have a copy you'd like to donate. . .

Those books may reflect the more baleful consequences of Union's long pre-coeducational history. The consequences of the campus being situated to catch every February breeze are on the whole healthier:

North of North College
The Arctic theme would of course begin with William Henry Seward (Class of 1820) who was responsible for the purchase of Alaska (having earlier declined to purchase Cuba, which presumably did not remind him so strongly of *alma mater*).

Sheldon Jackson (Class of 1855), a Presbyterian missionary, became U.S. Superintendent of Public Instruction for Alaska, and wrote a couple books on that Territory. His annual reports on *The Introduction of Domesticated Reindeer into Alaska*, published for 15 years by the Government Printing Office, record one of the more unusual (and important) contributions of Union's alumni to the public welfare: the Eskimo were fast running out of things to eat.

Finding the first of those reports, published in 1890, and the 1896 report, would complete the library's holdings of this series.

A recent gift to the Library from an anonymous Friend adds to the Arctic theme, and is interesting in other ways. *Bob North with Dog Team and Indians*(1929) is by Robert Carver North (Class of 1936). The Library already owned several scholarly books by North, a Professor of Political

Science at Stanford, but had not suspected the existence of three books he wrote about his travels in northern Canada *before* attending Union. The book just received was written and published when the author was 14; still lacking are similar books he published in the two preceding years!

Precocious authorship could be another theme, and a natural one for the college that counts John Howard Payne, author of "Home, Sweet Home", among its honored alumni - Payne had a play produced in New York at fourteen, and entered Union later the same year.

But this game could go on indefinitely, and may give a false impression, because the day-to-day reality is that books come in, or are found, helter-skelter: patterns and themes only appear on detached reflection.

Can you find a common theme in the following recent acquisitions?

Butter and Lichens

From Dr. Kenneth Rappoport, a member of the Friends, came the gift of the 1888 letterbook of Chicago attorney William H. King (Class of 1846), a Trustee of the College (1887-92.) The correspondence concerns business, personal, and College affairs - ordering butter from Wisconsin (and protesting express charges of "almost two cents a pound"), buying, or not buying, farm land in North Dakota, dunning his clients, and most interesting to College historians, trying (unsuccessfully) to rally Trustee opinion against selection of former professor Harrison Webster as next President of Union. He couldn't attend the crucial meeting himself because a Hansom cab horse had stepped on his foot, (a neat inversion of "For want of a horse, a kingdom was lost").

A 1985 exhibition catalogue from the Benaki Museum in Athens includes several photographs by pioneering photographer William James Stillman (Class of 1848). It was a gift from one of its editors, who did research on Stillman in Union's Archives.

If the Union Worthies series were revived, botanist Edward Tuckerman (Class of 1837) would be an excellent candidate for inclusion. He made many important contributions to the field of lichenology, and was apparently a man who would go anywhere to see a new lichen. He did so much lichen hunting on Mount Washington that a ravine there was later named for him.

Most recently, the Library has obtained a 1978 publication entitled *Cryptogams of the U.S. North Pacific Exploring Expedition, 1853-56*, which includes a paper by Tuckerman.

One can wait for history to be written and then try to acquire it, as librarians usually have to do, or one can see that it gets written, which is what Professor David Peak of the Physics Department has been doing. At his urging, Edward Hafner (Class of 1940) has just written his recollections of *Physics at Union Fifty Years Ago*, and Professor Peak has given the library a photocopy of the ten page typescript. A highly praiseworthy project, and one that should be imitated in every department.

Considering how much Union Collection material arrives in the mail, by purchase or gift, and how much can be found if enough time is spent perusing antiquarian booksellers' catalogues, it would be understandable if the librarians concerne stayed close to their desks.

Fortunately, the library has at present an Archivist and a Bibliographer who understand the advantage of going wherever the books are - an enlightened attitude that resulted in the purchase a few months ago, at an antiquarian book fair in Hancock, Massachusetts, of an interesting William Henry Seward letter, which joins others in the manuscript collections.

"Under the (U-V Screened) Lights of Special Collections, We all Become Siblings"

Building such collections is a backward-facing occupation, but Union's faculty and alumni have certainly not ceased to write books. A few yards from the Seward letter resides *The Laboring Classes in Renaissance Florence* (1980) by Samuel K. Cohn (Class of 1971) which must represent, in this sampling, all the future books which will one day burst into view like small towns seen from the rear platform of a fast train.

It's fun, if you're alert.

Wayne Somers
Chairman

FROM THE LIBRARIAN'S DESK

Projects and Collections

Happy 1987! Since I last addressed the Friends through the pages of the Newsletter, another busy and productive year at the Union College Library has slipped away. You will have to take my word that it was, indeed, a busy and productive year, because I do not propose to bore you with reports and statistics. Nevertheless I would like to describe some recent and important happenings.

Over the summers of 1985 and 1986, there were two major construction projects within Schaffer Library. One project took place in two phases over both summers. Both projects were made possible by generous financial support from the Schaffer Foundation.

Compact Shelving

Stack space for collection growth had been shrinking at an alarming rate over the last several years. This space shortage was especially severe on the Lower Level, where periodicals and government documents are housed.

The most viable solution to our problem was the installation of mobile compact shelving. Once funding for the purchase and installation of this shelving was secured from the Schaffer Foundation, contract negotiations were undertaken with the chosen vendor, and work began immediately following Commencement.

Both phases required the removal of the old stacks, temporary relocation of the collections and the furniture, construction of a false floor with its rails, and erection of the new compact shelving. At the same time, new carpeting was laid down, and the areas were repainted. In both summers, the projects were finished on schedule, and the stacks were re-opened to public use by the beginning of the Fall Terms

Renovated Phi Beta Kappa Area

During the summer of 1986, a major renovation of the west (front) end of Schaffer Library, affecting the first through the fourth floors, got underway. The Phi Beta Kappa room and the adjacent area of the third floor were redesigned and handsomely refurnished in memory of Mr. and Mrs. Henry Schaffer, the Library's major benefactors.

As part of the design, new bookcases were built to house the Bigelow Collection and various memorabilia from the professional and personal life of Henry Schaffer. Additional access to the new area was gained by the construction of a splendid staircase.

The new area is comfortable and conducive to study and is consequently very popular with the students. When you next visit the campus, please come in to see this most elegant addition to the Library.

Recent Special Acquisitions

Now that I've written briefly about things physical, I'd like to turn, equally briefly, to things bibliographical. In our continuing effort to strengthen our collection of modern first editions, Special Collections has acquired for the Rare Book Collection three William Faulkner works: *A Fable, The Town* and *The Mansion*; T. S. Eliot's *Notes Toward a Definition of Culture*; Wallace Stevens' *The Auroras of Autumn*, and Eudora Welty's *The Golden Apples*.

Our Pre-Raphaelite holdings were increased by the addition of three books by Christina Rossetti: *A Pageant, The Prince's Progress and other Poems*, and *Goblin Market and other Poems*. The volumes are uniformly bound by Zaehnsdorf in blue leather with gilt decorations and blue marbled endpapers. *The Prince's Progress* and *Goblin Market* each have two lovely designs, the frontispiece and the title page by Dante Gabriel Rossetti.

Grayson's Birds

The single most impressive acquisition for the Rare Book Collection this past year was Andrew Jackson Grayson's *Birds of the Pacific Slope*, published by Arion Press. Grayson, an artist-naturalist of the mid-nineteenth century, deliberately set out to follow the example of Audubon and paint the birds of the Far West, which Audubon had never visited. The work reproduces in full scale all Grayson's surviving paintings in the Bancroft Library of the University of California at Berkeley.

As Union College Library's most prized possession is the elephant folio of Audubon's *Birds of America*, bought by Eliphalet Nott from the artist himself, our purchase of *Birds of the Pacific Slope* seemed most appropriate. These two works complement each other most effectively.

Let me emphasize, as I do so often, how important the Special Collections are as a part of the Library's role in the education of students. Exposure to such beautiful and rare volumes enriches the lives of all who come in contact with them. The contribution of the Friends in support of the Special Collections is a major one, and we are indeed most grateful for your continued interest.

Ann Seemann
Librarian

THE SCHENECTADY ARCHIVES OF SCIENCE AND TECHNOLOGY

In November of 1970 the Bibliographer of Schaffer Library (whose identity is revealed elsewhere in this newsletter) wrote a memo to Dr. Edwin K. Tolan, the Librarian, proposing the formation of a new special collection which would contain the personal papers and manuscripts of Schenectady-based electrical engineers and scientists. The Library already owned the papers of such well known electrical scientists as Charles P. Steinmetz, Ernst Alexanderson, Ernst Berg, Samuel Nixdorff, and Birger Nordlander.

During the next few years Dr. Tolan pursued the idea of the establishment of an "archives" of science and technology with members of the Union College faculty and administration, representatives from industry, and historians of science. In April of 1976 the Schenectady Archives of Science and Technology was formally dedicated. Unfortunately, Dr. Tolan had passed away two months before the opening of the Archives. The Schenectady Archives of Science and Technology (SAST) remains in existence today as a memorial to his diligence and foresight

The years since the formal creation of the SAST have seen a remarkable growth in the size of this special collection. Personal papers and manuscripts from Edwin W. Rice, Jr., Philip Alger, Frederick Grover, Gabriel Kron, William E. Ruder, Kenneth Kingdon, Albert Hull, Frank Elder, Clarence Hewlett, William Stanley and others have been added to the Schenectady Archives of Science and Technology in the past eleven years. The collection now occupies about five hundred linear feet of space.

A cursory glance at any of the collections in the SAST would reveal a seemingly motley array of blueprints, correspondence, technical formulas, photographs, computer print-outs, reprints of technical articles, etc. Several of the collections need further arranging and describing, and this is a very time consuming process. But it is important to remember that each of the collections makes a contribution to the history of electrical science.

Who conducts research with these papers and manuscripts and for what purposes do they use them? I have seen the SAST papers used in a variety of ways. Materials from the Steinmetz Papers have been included in several recent doctoral dissertations. The Alexanderson and Westinghouse (an informal member of the SAST group) collections have been used as sources for undergraduate papers and a thesis. Letters from Oliver Heaviside (the author of an early twentieth century calculus text) to Ernst J. Berg are part of the Berg Papers and a recent gift from the IEEE. These letters were recently used by a researcher writing a biography of Heaviside.

Ernst Alexanderson's papers include a large quantity of material on his pioneering work in the development of television. This has been used by several people working on the history of television and by one person who wanted to build a working replica of Alexanderson's television camera. A GE engineer has examined the Alexanderson and Hewlett papers for his paper on the technical history of the thyratron.

The Ernst Berg papers have provided scholars with biographical data on Steinmetz. Berg was also a faculty member at Union and succeeded Steinmetz as head of the Electrical Engineering Department. His papers contain a great deal of information on various aspects of the teaching of electrical engineering at Union. These portions of the Berg papers are useful not only to historians of science but also to historians of Union College.

This list does not exhaust all of the uses for which I have seen the SAST employed, but the picture is clear: The Schenectady Archives of Science and Technology is used by researchers from a variety of academic and nonacademic backgrounds for a wide array of purposes.

When the SAST was established, the founders hoped to create a collection of personal papers and manuscripts from local, i.e. Schenectady area, scientists with national recognition in the field of electrical science and electrical engineering. This scientific archive would, in the words of the Schaffer Library bibliographer, "... represent the merger of history and electrical engineering." The problems posed by new media (magnetic tape, disk, floppy disk, etc.) which may be encountered with future additions to the SAST have yet to be solved. Nevertheless, the collection has fulfilled the promise of its founders. It continues to grow and to be used.

I came to Schaffer Library in 1979 as an archivist with a solid nontechnical (read "nonscientific") background. The technical details of alternators, thyratrons, the atomic bomb, and even television were unknown to me. In spite of my scientific ignorance, I have been looking at the collections in the SAST for the past seven years. Sometimes this "looking" was done to help a researcher use a particular collection, and sometimes I did it simply to increase my knowledge of the collections. My few years of contact with the collections in the Schenectady Archives of Science and Technology have slightly diminished the aforementioned ignorance and have convinced me that this collection and others like it are significant sources for the history of science and technology in the twentieth century.

Ellen Fladger
Archivist

SOME NOTES ON THE HISTORY OF UNION'S SPECIAL COLLECTIONS

"But she doesn't know how lucky she is!" I thought when I read Ellen Fladger's account in last year's Newsletter of a busy week in the Special Collections Department. The opportunities and possibilities inherent in Special Collections have always interested me and I remember how far from ideal their arrangements were, both in Schaffer Library before the addition of 1974, and in the Nott Memorial before Schaffer Library opened in 1961. Since Ellen lets me into her bailiwick on occasion, my envy is not long-lasting. But I began to think about where the parts that now constitute the entity called Special Collections were housed and how difficult it was to use them.

Alumni who studied in the "round building' may remember the Rare Books in their glass-fronted cases against the west wall of the main floor. The Union, Bailey, Bigelow and Schenectady Collections, inhabiting the mezzanine, in caged alcoves with grill-work doors, were very tempting to amateur locksmiths. The Vault in the basement, with its heavy, safe-deposit-like door, must have aroused a certain curiosity among students until the area in front of that door was converted into additional storage space. This simple cage of 2 x 4's and screening largely blocked the view of the Vault. As a matter of fact, it was difficult to see the contents even when one was in the Vault--a single bulb in the ceiling augmented by another single bulb on a long cord provided the only light.

A good share of the College's archival material was put in the Vault after being rescued in the early 1930's from the attic over Old Chapel and from the third floor of the Nott Memorial, a huge, dusty, unheated area not entirely safe from leaks in the roof. Not all of this material had been catalogued or classified, and it was always a challenge to try to locate the necessary document or volume.

With the 1961 move to the Schaffer Library, most of the Union Collection and archives, together with the Schenectady Collection and the Bailey Collection, were brought together for the first time in one room. That room was clean and secure, but lacked any climate control beyond a portable dehumidifier, and it had only one table for work space. In the late '60's, after the acquisition of the Alexanderson papers, this room became crowded. In another room, several dozen filing cabinets of historic letters engaged for a while in a territorial dispute with the College's telephone switching equipment.

The completion of the addition in 1974 permitted consolidation of all these collections on the fourth floor. Until then Rare Books were divided between some large bookcases on the third floor and shelving in the Librarian's Office, where they baked during part of each sunny day.

Although I can remember the locations of these collections, I had no accurate idea of their origin or history. A quick search pointed up a need for the Library to organize the facts of its own growth; the information is there but scattered through several sets of records. The Bailey Collection of American Wit and Humor proved easiest to trace; it had been given by Frank Bailey, long the College's treasurer and benefactor, in 1921. Books were added over the years when he found additional titles and the librarians suggested titles to him.

Rare Books were harder to pin down; many of them were acquired, one at a time, by gift, or else simply emerged from the Library's general collection. In an article for a 1925 issue of the *Union Alumni Monthly*, Wharton Miller, Librarian from 1921 to 1927, discussed some books he considered interesting and probably rare. He did not mention where these rare books were shelved; but a few old handwritten cards in the card catalogue suggest they were in the "Librarian's Alcove." We are not, however, quite sure what that was or how it was supervised.

The books on Miller's list are all still in Schaffer Library, sixty-two years later, although the first volume of Audubon's *Birds of America* was stolen in 1971 and lost for a month before its recovery, an event that heightened the Library's awareness of the need to protect its rare books. Long-time Friends will remember John Jenkins and his account of the "Audubon Caper" (his term, not ours).

Mr. Miller also noted in his article that he was trying to collect any items having to do with Union and its graduates. He urged alumni to send him any Unioniana with which they were willing to part. He offered to acquire bookcases for this material and maintain the cases and their contents in a special alcove. For several years the *Union Alumni Monthly* recorded the progress of his efforts; the last article before he left Union noted ten bookcases, almost full. These oak cases would seem to be the formal start of the Union Collection, which now fills about 150 shelves and 25 file drawers.

More research needs to be done on the establishment of the Schenectady Collection and on the retrieval of the First Purchase books from the general stacks.

The First Purchase collection comprises those books still in the Library's possession which were chosen by the Trustees at their first meeting in 1795 and ordered from a Philadelphia bookseller. The bookseller in turn imported many of them from London. The Trustees authorized payment in 1796, again listing the books in their *Minutes*. There are thus several, occasionally conflicting, authorities for designating books as "First Purchase". Exactly when the tracing of these items and their separation from the general collection began is unclear, but it has proved to be an ongoing process with an occasional First Purchase still turning up in the stacks.

The Special Collections are now overflowing the space on the fourth floor, space seemingly sufficient in 1974. Ms. Fladger is indeed still "lucky" by the standards of my experience from 1952 to 1974. Nonetheless, and despite very careful judgments on acquisitions, the Collections are again reaching the multi-locational stage. Plus ça change...

Ruth Anne Evans
Associate Librarian

NEWSLETTER

ARCHIVES AND SPECIAL COLLECTIONS AT COLGATE UNIVERSITY

Volume 1   Fall 1986   Number 1

ARCHIVIST'S COLUMN

The University Archives/Special Collections (UA/SC) Department houses the records of Colgate University as well as other specialized collections including rare books, ephemera, manuscripts, posters, and other print and non-print materials. The Department is responsible for the collection and preservation of, and access to these materials. The Department is administered by the University Archivist.

The Department is located in the Case Library on the second floor. The hours of operation have been recently extended to better serve the university community. They are 9:00 a.m. until 9:00 p.m. Monday through Thursday, 9:00 a.m. until 5:00 p.m. on Friday and 1:00 until 6:00 p.m. on Sunday. During the summer and between semesters the hours are 9:00 a.m. until 4:00 p.m. All requests for use of the UA/SC outside scheduled hours will be handled on an individual basis.

The UA/SC has over 6000 cubic feet of materials, including approximately 11,000 volumes. In the current reorganization it has been divided into seven main divisions. The UNIVERSITY ARCHIVES contain non-current records of Colgate University, preserved because of their continuing value, and include the Faculty and Alumni Papers, the Biographical, Class, and Buildings and Grounds Files, and most student and University publications.

The UNIVERSITY ARCHIVES: SPECIAL COLLECTIONS designates materials not grouped with the paper records acquired through transfer. This includes photographs, museum pieces, artifacts, ephemera, and other university memorabilia. The RARE BOOKS AND MANUSCRIPTS division separates those items stored in the vault area.

The UA/SC in the Case Library houses many materials related to athletics at Colgate. A separate collection is housed in the Huntington Gymnasium and staffed by the athletic department. Together they form the ATHLETIC ARCHIVES. Inquiries concerning athletics can be addressed to the University Archives.

There are many individual collections with a literary theme. These materials, such as the Joseph Conrad, John C. Powys, and Ernest Gann collections make up the SPECIAL COLLECTIONS: LITERARY DIVISION.

Materials about New York State and Hamilton and its vicinity are included in the SPECIAL COLLECTIONS: STATE AND LOCAL DIVISION. These include the railroad collections, and other materials mainly dealing with farm and industrial areas.

The final division deals with SPECIAL COLLECTIONS: TOPICAL. This division covers those collections that do not fit into other categories. The World War I and II Poster Collection, the Early Modern London Collection, the Orrin E. Dunlap Collection of Early Radio, Radar, and Television History are examples from this division.

The Department provides administrative and educational/research services. Records management represents a substantial part of the services provided by the Department to the university community.

The UA/SC serve not only as an information resource but also as a learning and research laboratory. By using primary, unusual, and rare materials, students gain an educational experience not available through the use of secondary sources. They are introduced to the various collections, avenues of research and the techniques and procedures for the use of Special Collections.

The Department provides instruction in the finding of information. The University Archivist gives general and subject lectures on the uses of primary research materials, as well as areas such as the history of the book, printing and binding history, the antiquarian book trade, conservation, and other areas. In January of 1987 and perhaps each January thereafter a course entitled "An Introduction to Historical and Contemporary Manuscripts and Archival Documents" will be offered. With the Department's assistance, students write papers on some aspect of the collections or help to develop finding aids and process collections.

An internship program for students interested in research in the UA/SC and/or considering a career in the fields of Archives, Rare Book Librarianship, Special Collections Administration, conservation or Museum Studies is planned.

The UA/SC Department is in charge of Exhibits throughout the libraries and a museum display in the UA/SC museum room. Also, programs concerning the collections and UA/SC programs are available.

The UA/SC Department not only preserves, protects and makes accessible materials but also has an active collection program. This includes the transfer of archival materials to the Department. It also includes the acquisition of University memorabilia, rare books, and Special Collections. The University accepts donations of these materials for their preservation and scholarly use. Suitable collections or single items should be brought to the attention of the University Archivist and their possible acquisition discussed.

University students and faculty, genealogists, students of local history and literature and other researchers are encouraged to use the collections.

In the Spring issue of the Newsletter recent acquisitions will be highlighted. In addition to the columns in the Fall issue there will be a section on Conservation at Colgate.

EXHIBITS

The UA/SC in conjunction with the Psychology Department's Centennial Celebration opened exhibits in the Libraries and Olin Hall on the history of Psychology at Colgate. These exhibits are still on view.

An exhibit on Railroads in New York is on display in the main lobby of the Case Library.

UPCOMING EXHIBITS

In January, 1987 the Museum Room of the UA/SC will have an exhibit entitled, "Americana: 1910-1930." This will feature materials from the Weiner, Wilson, Archives, and Poster Collections.

This Newsletter is a joint publication of the Archives and the Friends of the Library. For information contact the University Archivist, Case Library, Colgate University, Hamilton, New York 13346. (315) 824-1000, Ext. 305

FRIENDS OF THE COLGATE UNIVERSITY LIBRARY

The Friends of the Library, in its twenty-seventh year, welcomes new members to its executive committee. Catherine Trout and Lucia Blackmore, and of course the new University Librarian, Judith Green, have joined us, with Richard Frost as Secretary and G. David Anderson as Treasurer. Our fall agenda has included plans for expansion of the organization as well as the usual business of purchasing books that will enhance Colgate's collection, but which fall outside the purview of the regular budget for acquisitions. Our greatest coup this season has been Joseph Slater's find of the out-of-print Works of James Fenimore Cooper, illustrated by Felix O. Darley (Townsend, 1859-61), 32 volumes.

The Friends' annual "Books and Coffee" will take place in the Jerome Room, Wednesday, January 21, at 4:00 P.M. The speaker will be Jill Harsin, Assistant Professor of History, who is teaching a course on "Love and Marriage among the Victorians" as part of the January Special Studies Period. Her subject will be cognate with the course. Each January, the Friends seek a speaker who will draw the Hamilton community as well as the student community, and Professor Harsin's talk seems ideally suited to this synthetic task.

We have engaged Frederick Busch, Fairchild Professor of English, to speak at the annual meeting and luncheon in April, 1987. Professor Busch had lately experienced a new aspect of the fiction-writing trade: the process of having his novel Rounds wooed by agents, producers, and filmmakers. He will entertain the Friends and their guests with the literary and economic vicissitudes of this adventure.

Membership in the Friends

We take this opportunity to invite renewal of membership, life membership, and especially new membership in our organization. The recent "reforms" in tax law may make a donation to the Friends before the end of the year a timely choice. A membership form is attached to this edition of the Newsletter for your use.

A further fundraising note: Gordon McGregor, Assistant Professor of French at Colgate from 1975 until 1981, died on August 30, 1986. In memory of him and the interest in literature, especially comparative and contemporary literature, he sustained among several "generations" of Colgate students, a book fund has been established. The collection will emphasize literary biography and contemporary fiction and poetry. Contributions to the Gordon D. McGregor Memorial Book Fund can be sent to Ronald Joyce, Director of Development, Colgate University, Hamilton, New York, 13346.

               Deborah J. Knuth, President
Friends of the Colgate University Library

Everett Needham Case Library

TRADITIONS

One of the oldest and most fondly remembered traditions at Colgate is the Mercury Legend. The Mercury statue "The Bird" was a presence at Colgate from about 1890 until the early 1920's.

It was originally a piece of art, a bronze statue of Mercury donated by an alumnus to the University. However, the bronze washed away in the rain leaving a rather unlovely creature.

The students clowned with the statue, dressing it and generally calling attention to its unworthiness.

It was decided that the statue was a disgrace as an art object but might be useful in the way of Amherst's "Sabrina". A tradition was begun to create a feeling of class loyalty.

Complicated rules were drawn up. Mercury would be in the possession of a class. Even-numbered classes would hold the statue for a year, then attempt to pass it to the next even-numbered class. The odd-numbered classes would attempt to capture it and pass it to the next odd-numbered class.

During the year, the statue had to be shown at the first class banquet and at a Spring athletic event. It was allowed to be stored indoors only for brief times when not on display.

The odd-numbered or out class would use these display times to attempt to capture the Bird. They would crash banquets that were held in secret. They would sneak around at night trying to discover the statue being moved. They would plot and plan and try to outguess their opponents.

The rivalry became heated and techniques of moving and secreting it became more involved over the thirty years that the tradition persisted. Early classes displayed Mercury from houses and buried the Bird in back yards. Treks through the woods and chartered trains were common. Wild goose chases were mounted. Later times saw Mercury sent through the mail, taken to New York City, stored in safe deposit boxes. Eventually, the competition seemed to get out of hand. The arrival of the automobile led to car races. At one point gun shots were fired during a chase.

The administration decided too much time and energy were being expended on this whim. The possibility of violence was a concern. Consequently, Mercury was retired by the Class of 1921.

Parts of the Bird were melted into coins and given to various class members. The rest of the broken parts were taken up by interested parties. The statue all but disappeared.

Reed Alvord, class of 1931, later discovered the head of the Mercury and the class of 1931 presented it to the Alumni Corporation. It was displayed in the Alumni office until 1986. At present, the head and several other parts, donated by Bill Wilson, Class of 1920, are on display in the University Archives. Eventually, it might be fun to try to put Mercury back together again. We are always looking for the missing parts and are interested in Mercury lore.

Article by Merle vonWettberg

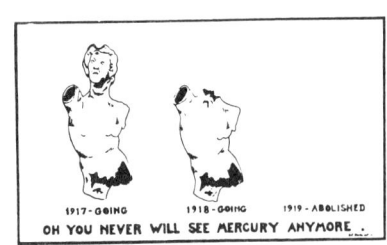

OH YOU NEVER WILL SEE MERCURY ANYMORE.

The Passing of Mercury

VOL. I NO. 1
SUMMER 1985

Newsletter of the Friends of the Wellesley College Library

Beginning a long and fruitful friendship...

Greetings:

Honorary Chairperson
Nannerl O. Keohane '61

Founding Member
Mary Jackson '24

Honorary Member
Helen Hooven Santmyer '18

Co-Chairpersons
Eleanor A. Gustafson
Suzanne C. Mueller '46

Steering Committee
Anne Anninger
Jean Glasscock '33
Emiko I. Nishino '45
Cynthia D. Post '34
Helene K. Sargeant '40
Doris P. Scheff '49
Kathleen H. Strehle '63
Jeanne P. Robertson '55
Helen L. Robertson '61
Janet R. Tulloss '48

Advisory Committee
Ruth F. Boorstein '38
Nardi R. Campion '38
Y. T. Feng
Vartan Gregorian
Eleanor Gustafson
Jay Lucker
Thomas O'Connell
Frank Streeter
Alice R. True '35
Leah Rose Werthan '29
George Whitney

Helen Hooven Santmyer '18 reminisces with Betty K. F. Johnson '44. (story on page 2)

The Friends of Wellesley College Library has come into being, thanks to you, the membership."Affection," "esteem," and "support," all characteristics of friendship in the view of Mr. Webster, have been proferred by over 200 charter friends – and each day brings another envelope in the mail. We thank each of you for your interest and your vote of confidence.

In addition to support received from library buffs worldwide (our membership comes from 26 states of the Union, England and Hong Kong), Wellesley alumnae have rallied about to make the dream of President Keohane and Mary Jackson a reality. A Steering Committee has been recruited and has met to map plans and procedures. Later an Advisory Council will inject a note of professional advice and direction. There's room and need aplenty for help should you wish to be a part of this enterprise; we encourage you to take the initiative to write.

The present membership of the Friends of the Library will remain so for the calendar year 1985. Renewals will be sought annually starting in 1986. We urge you to help us enlarge our rolls by passing this bulletin along to a fellow alumna or by bringing a potential member to one of our scheduled events.

An inaugural meeting at the time of the Alumnae Leadership Council held in October 1984 found David Ives, Trustee of the College and Vice-Chairman of the WGBH Foundation, sharing some thoughts on Wellesley's library from the speaker's podium in the Chapel. Afterwards, under sparkling blue skies, our first "friends" gathered on the Library Terrace to celebrate the occasion with a libation.

Two quite different events took place this spring: one a lecture highlighting a special exhibit of cookbooks, the other a fete at Harvard's Houghton Library honoring one of the most distinguished curators on the Library staff.

As we go about our plans, it seems evident that there are unlimited ways to develop a Friends program, for Wellesley's library is an organization of great distinction and utility, a vital component of the College's educational process and excellence. If we can illuminate the scope and elegance of the Library, reaffirm the centrality of it and its resources to the work of the students and faculty, and develop a fuller understanding of its potential and needs, we will have gone a long way toward achieving our goals for the Friends. That this may happen in congenial, stimulating and entertaining circumstances is just one of the bonuses that come from the impulse to advance the purposes of the College, and in this particular instance a most important part of it, the Library.

Eleanor A. Gustafson
Suzanne C. Mueller '46

MARY JACKSON '24 MAKES FOUNDING GIFT

Mary E. Jackson '24 of Shaker Heights, Ohio, backed her belief in the value of organizing a Friends of the Library with a gift of $10,000 seed money. In appreciation, a citation, exquisitely executed in calligraphy by Marilyn Hatch, Special Collections Assistant, was delivered to Miss Jackson at her home by Janet Sloan '56 and Martha Schauss '40. These two very able ambassadors of Wellesley who make calls on alumnae less able to journey to the campus had earlier visited Miss Jackson and learned of her strong conviction that a Friends group would strengthen the Library program.

They described their visit: "Miss Mary Jackson '24, small and decorous, receives callers in the parlor of her gracious old family home. She is surrounded by Victorian furniture and lovely glass-shaded lamps. In the sunlight, the prisms cast little rainbows about the room.

Mary Jackson is still every inch a librarian. When asked to become the Founding Member, she, in turn, asked detailed questions about the plans. She likes to be precise. She wanted to know about special lectures, new and important acquisitions, and special activities which would be supported by Friends of the Library. She feels that the library is the heart and soul of a liberal arts college.

(continued on back page)

119

A VISIT WITH THE LADY OF THE CLUB

Twenty years ago, Katherine Wright sent me a copy of *Ohio Town* with a note saying, "This Wellesley writer is a classmate and a neighbor. I know you will relish these essays. I hope she writes more." I did, and she did. In the fall of 1983, *And The Ladies of the Club* made its spectacular appearance. Helen Hooven Santmyer '18 had earlier seen the novel published to little acclaim. Now it was a major event: Book of the Month selection and a TV mini-series. Notice of its republication appeared on the front page of the *New York Times*. Since then, *Ohio Town* has been republished as well, and *The Ladies* has enjoyed a long stay on the Bestsellers' Lists.

In the wake of the TV crews and newspaper reporters, Nancy Agnew and I went to interview Miss Santmyer in Xenia. We stopped first at the single frame house which had been home for most of the 88 years of this author whose remarkable success in her ninth decade had stirred the fibre of repressed writers across America. On the edge of town in a sunny spacious retirement community, we were greeted by pleasant personnel happily adjusted to the extraordinary media attention to their senior citizen. Coffee was ready and Miss Santmyer awaited us in her wheel chair, freshly coiffed, bright eyed, and sparkling in Christmas colored silk.

We had a jovial time, talking about the Wellesley she knew. Nancy had brought a 1918 year book to prompt a memory which needed no spur. Her recollection of Wellesley was complete, whole. She was grateful for the reading and writing she had done, had sharp humorous vignettes of the professors who had taught her: Hart, Denkinger, Sherwood, Shackford, and Perkins. Her membership in Scribblers, directed by Miss Lockwood, and in AKX, and regular sessions writing under trees on the golf course

Home of Helen Hooven Santmyer

(later reporting remarkable scores for the time spent) developed a skill which later she was to teach and practice.

Miss Santmyer's Wellesley years had been wholly shadowed by the First World War as mine had been by the Second. She did not think the College was as caught up in the First as in the Second, Imperial Germany being less hateful than the Nazi menace. Her life after Wellesley was circumscribed by Ohio, save for brief intervals: a B. Litt at Oxford and a period in New York City.

The massive public response to her lately recognized writing she dismisses as ninety percent because she is nearly ninety. One had the sense of a patient woman accepting humorously the natural vicissitudes of age and modestly accepting praise, which might well have come decades earlier, with grace and no irony.

Betty K. F. Johnson '44
Cincinnati, Ohio

Editor's note: Betty Johnson is Chairman of the Board of Trustees of Wellesley, and Nancy Agnew, Director of Publications. Katherine Timberman Wright '18 served Wellesley as Trustee for 18 years, after terms of office as Chairman of the National Development Fund and President of the Alumnae Association. Mrs. Wright died in the summer of 1984.

DESIDERATA...

Two years ago, James O'Gorman, Professor of Art at Wellesley, gave the Library a handsome collection of books illustrated by Hammatt Billings. Since then, Anne Anninger has been trying to build up the holdings of 19th century American illustrated books and to complete holdings of 19th century French. Both American and French are used on a regular basis by the Art Department. There follows a list of books that would be greatly welcomed by the Library. Is there one resting in your library – or in your attic?

London, a Pilgrimage
by Blanchard Jerrold.
Illustrated by Gustave Doré.
London, Unwin, Grant & Co., 1872.

Le Charivari.
Paris, 1832-38.
(Any issue).

La Caricature, journal fondé et dirigé par C. Philipon.
Paris, Aubert, 1830-35.
(Any issue).

Voyages Pittoresques et Romantiques dans l'Ancienne France
by Isidore J. S. Taylor. 1820-1845. 23 v.
(Any of the volumes).

Books illustrated by O.C. Darley

Major Jones's Courtship
by William T. Thompson. 2nd Edition.
Philadelphia, Carey and Hart, 1844.

Peter Ploddy, and Other Oddities
by Joseph C. Neal.
Philadelphia, Carey and Hart, 1844.

The Book of the Army, comprising a General History of the United States
by John Frost.
New York, D. Appleton & Co. 1845.

Chronicles of Pineville, embracing sketches of Georgia Scenes, Incidents, and Characters
by the Author of
"Major Jones's Courtship"
Philadelphia, Carey and Hart, 1845.

Moral Tales
by Maria Edgeworth.
Philadelphia, George S. Appleton, 1845. 3 v.

NEW YORK TIMES FOOD WRITER WHETS WELLESLEY APPETITES

Marian Fox Burros—Class of '54

Marian Fox Burros, graduating in 1954, when raising children and arranging flowers was the usual feminine route, followed it, but soon cooked her way out of the house. With never a thought to becoming a journalist, within 10 years, she was Food Editor of the Washington Post and is now a Food Critic for the New York Times, often dubbed "the Ralph Nader of the food World."

The beginning was an index card file of recipes which grew into the self-published *Elegant, but Easy*, now a classic. Seven cookbooks later (five written with fellow alumna, Lois Levine '52), Burros says Wellesley taught her all the things she needed to know to become a journalist. Liberal arts, she says, prepare one for the world – "practical things come later" – but English Comp trained her to think rationally, to understand, and to explore.

Marian Fox Burros had not been back to the campus since the early '60's, but she returned at the invitation of the Friends of the Library to lecture, appropriately enough in conjunction with a special display of rare cookbooks and herbals in March. The politics of food absorb Burros's attention these days more than recipes or eating (2 years on assignment grading New York restaurant fare kept her "eating out" six nights a week – "the weight I gained!"). She is indeed an investigative reporter, researching food safety (red #3 coloring, antibiotics in animal feed), consumerism, nutrition, but has not lost her zest and humor which is manifested in her column "De Gustibus," appearing Saturdays on the Op Ed page of the NY Times. A recent column explores people's likes and dislikes in tunafish sandwiches.

Mrs. Burros's lecture was the first formal event arranged for the Friends of the Library and was a delight to all who attended. It was preceded by an elegant luncheon at the College Club attended by members of the Steering Committee. Tea, coffee, wine, and delicious tid-bits were served following the lecture. You can be sure that the food was of a standard to merit kudos from the eminent critic!

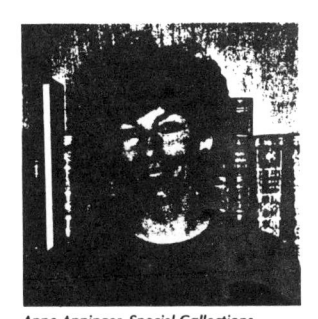

Anne Anninger, Special Collections Librarian

ANNINGER HONORED AT HOUGHTON

On April 9, Anne Anninger, Wellesley Library's Special Collections Librarian, gave a gallery tour of the show of *Spanish and Portuguese Illustrated Books of the 16th Century* at the Houghton Library, Harvard University. Formerly cataloguer for Printing and Graphic Arts there, Anne prepared the exhibition and composed the catalogue and bibliography, basing her descriptions on her personal acquaintance with the collection.

Houghton took the opportunity to gild the occasion by inviting the Friends of Wellesley College Library to attend, making it a real party by serving elegant refreshments. Wellesley has reason for pride in its Special Collections and in their curator.

RECENT LIBRARY EVENTS

In celebration of Black History Month, all through February, there was a display of recent Special Collections acquisitions in Black Studies. On February 20, Anne Anninger also led a discussion on the historical sequence of literature written for and about Blacks, depicting stereotypes and racist attitudes of the period.

★

Also during February and through March 15, there was an exhibit arranged by Ross Wood in the Music Library in honor of the 300th anniversary of the birth of George Frideric Handel (1685-1739) which included rare editions of works both by and about the famous composer.

★

★

During February and March, Susan Barbarossa mounted a fascinating exhibition of cookbooks and herbals from the Special Collections called "Larks, Lead, and Lice: Meals and Medicines from the Past." It was to highlight this display that the Friends of the Library arranged for Marian Fox Burros '54, New York Times Food Editor, to speak to members on March 6. A report of this appears above.

★

On March 14, Colin Franklin of the London publishers, Kegan Paul, spoke on "Books as Art," in the Lecture Room. A prolific author, Mr. Franklin has published the most important history of private presses since Ramson's 1929 work. He is presently at work editing the papers of the Ashendene Press.

★

In celebration of the bicentennial of the birth of John James Audubon, 1785-1851, the New York, 1860 edition of *The Birds of America* was on display in Special Collections during the month of April.

★

GIRLS GOSSIP: LETTERS OF ELIZABETH BARRETT BROWNING TO A FRIEND

Three volumes of letters between two young women who used to write to each other at least twice a week are an event of the current publishing scene. The writers were Elizabeth Barrett Browning and Mary Russell Mitford whose faithful correspondence scanned the years between 1838 and 1854. The editors are Meredith B. Raymond and Mary Rose Sullivan, who worked over a period of ten years in the Wellesley College Library on the project.

Miss Mitford described the letters as "really talk, fireside talk, neither better nor worse, assuming a form of permanence-gossip daguerreotyped." We are now able to eavesdrop on their gossip which covers practically all the opinions, preoccupations, topics, and scandals that set the tongues of England's intelligentsia wagging during the first two decades of Queen Victoria's reign.

For anyone interested in Elizabeth Barrett Browning, the importance of these letters cannot be overemphasized. They encompass some of the most significant developments and events in her life: her "exile" to Torquay for health reasons; the drowning there of her favorite brother, a tragedy for which she felt responsible; her acquisition, from Miss Mitford, of the renowned dog Flush; publication of her *Poems* (1844), which led to her acquaintance with Robert Browning; her marriage to Browning and their flight to Italy; her sorrowful estrangement from her father; the birth of her adored son; and, of course, her continuing poetical development.

Elizabeth admitted that once she began to write it was difficult to stop – comparing herself to "that bewitched broom in the story, which, being sent to draw water, drew bucket after bucket, until the whole house was in flood." In all, 497 letters – the largest number she wrote to a single correspondent – have been traced.

Wellesley College is one of the publishers of the three volumes, joining the Armstrong Browning Library, The Browning Institute and Wedgestone Press.

The Library's famous Browning collection was gathered in part by Wellesley President Alice Freeman Palmer. Following President Palmer's death, the collection was given to Wellesley by her husband as a memorial to his wife. Mr. Palmer also gave funds for additions to the collection. In 1930, Wellesley's 5th president, Caroline Hazard, gave the College the caskets which contained the Brownings' love letters. Books and manuscripts are now housed in Special Collections, in the Clapp Library, behind the original door of the Barrett's house on Wimpole Street. A substantial number of unpublished manuscripts are included and the collection is therefore of major interest to anyone writing now about the Brownings. A second edition of their poems and letters is underway in England, for example, and its editor is eager to work with Wellesley material.

The Browning collection is supplemented by the Marks Collection, given by Jeannette Marks '99. Her special interest was the ancestors of Elizabeth Barrett Browning, particularly the generation who settled in Jamaica. Largely made up of documents, the collection also includes a small but choice number of books about Jamaica.

(Much of this article is from Nancy Agnew's "Book Lover's Delight" which appeared in the March issue of Realia.)

Elizabeth Barrett Browning from a miniature by Matilda Carter, 18--

JACKSON (continued)

Miss Jackson is impressed with new Freshman Writing Program. She ho— that the students, with heightened sk— will more likely consider careers in w— ing, editing, and library scholarship. S— anticipates that the special program w— promote these interests.

After graduation with a major English from Wellesley, Miss Jacks— earned a degree in Library Science fr— Case Western Reserve University. S— worked as a librarian in the Clevela— Heights Library until 1946 when she — tired in order to care for her pare— Nevertheless, she continued her p— fessional interest for many years as a v— unteer. She took charge of cataloguing the Church of the Covenant Library— Cleveland. Today she still serves one mo— ing a week in the church Thrift Shop. S— has always been an enthusiastic garde— and is active in the Garden Club.

Newsletter of the
Friends of the Amherst College Library
1985-1986

This year the Council invited a professor of history to speak to the spring assembly of the Friends after their annual dinner in the Merrill Dining Commons. Robert Gross of the Amherst College Department of American Studies spoke about the social history of reading in Concord, Massachusetts, as reflected in the development of its public library during the first century of the republic.

Here, printed with Professor Gross's permission, is an edited version of part of the research into the Concord library records on which his speech to the Friends was based:

In the voluminous archives of the Concord Free Public Library sits a modest yet intriguing document: the draft report of the standing committee of the Concord Social Library for the year 1840. A few paragraphs long, it gives a brief account of the affairs of the association during the previous twelve months, following a format that had become standard since the library's formation in 1821. Essentially, it is a summary of statistics — the size of the collection, the number of new additions, the circulation for the year — no different in style from any that had come before. But the report contains an additional statement: a recommendation to alter the collections policy. "There is a number of books...," observed the committee, "of a religious and theological character consisting chiefly of sermons, which have no circulation from year to year." These volumes had come down from the late eighteenth century, relics of an earlier library venture in the town. It was time to clear them off the shelves. Without a trace of sentiment or another word, the committee proposed to donate the works to the Unitarian Church, which was planning to establish a "Public Religious Library" for the benefit of the town. It was a novel and radical step — a forerunner of the policies of "de-accession" so controversial among librarians today.

What gives this report such interest is that it was composed by Ralph Waldo Emerson, who had served on the standing committee for the previous three years. This was, of course, the very moment when Emerson was emerging as the leader of New England Transcendentalism, the spokesman for the spirit of "newness" that was stirring among intellectuals throughout the region. How fitting, then, that the man who had summoned the American scholar to cast off bondage to the past, who had denounced "corpse-cold" religion at Harvard Divinity School, should propose to banish from the Concord library the dessicated sermons of a faded age! Unfortunately — but characteristically — Emerson had conservative second thoughts. The call for de-accession is crossed out on the manuscript; it never made its way into the official report. Another decade would pass before Emerson would raise the issue again — this time without a bold plan for getting rid of the old books.

© The Friends of the Amherst College Library 1986

Description: The Friends of the Amherst College Library publishes an annual copyrighted newsletter of approximately 30 pages. The booklet is cream-colored with black and red print (folded 9 x 7"). Sample contents include an edited version of a speech from a Friends lecture; poetry; articles about new and special acquisitions; a list of coming exhibitions; activities of Friends; a Friends membership list.

PUBLICATIONS

> The Friends of the Goddard Library at Clark University is pleased to announce the first title in the Bibliolog Imprint Series for publication in December 1982
>
> ## My Liberal Education
> ### By Alice C. Higgins
> #### With Wood Engravings by Barry Moser
>
> The Third in the Clarkson Lecture Series presented at Clark University in April 1982.
>
> When she was elected chairman of Clark University's Board of Trustees in 1967, Alice Higgins became the first woman in history to chair a private coeducational college or university board. Her personal account of this experience provides a thoughtful and thought-provoking view of a tumultuous period in academic history.
>
> "Barry Moser is perhaps the foremost wood engraver in America." *Newsweek* review.
>
> Limited to 250 copies for sale, numbered 1-250 and hand bound in soft French marble wrappers with printed label. Each copy includes two signed original prints by artist Barry Moser with one laid in and suitable for framing. All copies are signed by the author. 5¾" x 7½". 48 pp. First edition. Nos. 1-100, $50.00. All other copies (Nos. 101-250) $100.00.
>
> No charge for postage and handling when check accompanies order.
>
> Friends of the Goddard Library
> Clark University
> Worcester, Massachusetts 01610
> (617) 793-7574
>
> Fifty percent of purchase price may be considered a tax-deductible contribution to the Friends of the Goddard Library.

Description: The Friends of the Goddard Library publishes selected books. The announcement for My Liberal Education is an off-white card (8 1/2 x 5 1/2") with black print and a purple border.

FRIENDS OF THE UNION COLLEGE LIBRARY

Schaffer Library
Union College
Schenectady, New York 12308

PUBLICATIONS LIST

Prices are net, and do not include postage unless payment accompanies order

Allen, Neal W.
Advertisement. To the Publick. The lot of the moderate, 1770. 1967. 11p. Boards. Folding plate.

An essay based on the only known copy (here reproduced in facsimile) of a 1770 New York City broadside announcing the partial lifting by the merchants of that city of the boycott against English imports.

In very short supply 15.00

Evans, Ruth Anne.
The W. Wright Hawkes collection of Revolutionary War documents; a catalogue. 1968. XV, 48p. Wrappers.

The documents described include 50 letters by George Washington, and others by Alexander Hamilton, Philip Schuyler, John Jay, John Hancock, Nathanael Greene, Israel Putnam, George Clinton and John Adams.

6.00

Hoffmann, Banesh.
Unexpected rewards; remarks upon the dedication of the Schenectady Archives of Science and Technology. 1976. 36p. Wrappers.

The author of The Strange Story of the Quantum and Albert Einstein, creator and rebel describes some dramatic instances of discoveries in scientific archives.

4.00

Jensen, Merrill
The popular leaders of the American Revolution. 1968. 23p. Wrappers. Printed at the Stinehour Press.

An address on the occasion of the first exhibition of the W. Wright Hawkes collection of Revolutionary War Papers.

5.00

McCord, James.
With corroding fires: William Blake as poet, print-maker and painter; a descriptive catalogue of an exhibition held at Scribner Library, Skidmore College... and Schaffer Library, Union College... 1980. 56p. Wrappers.

An extensively annotated catalogue, with 12 plates, of 54 Blake items from several institutional and private collections.

5.00

Miller, Frances.
Catalogue of the William James Stillman Collection...with an introduction and bibliography by Barbara Rotundo. 1974. 251p. Wrappers.

Stillman (1828-1901) an artist ("the first American pre-Raphaelite"), founding editor of the first American art journal, diplomat and journalist (eventually the London Times' correspondent in Greece and Italy) knew many of the leading writers and artists of America and Europe. The approximately 600 items described in this catalogue include letters or other manuscripts by Ford Madox Brown, Robert Browning, Edward Burne-Jones, Francesco Crispi, W.F. Gladstone, W.D. Howells, J.R. Lowell, D.G. Rossetti, John Ruskin, Leslie Stephen and Emile Zola.

7.50

Olton, Charles S.
The perplexing interlude: Washington's defensive strategy in 1777. 1971. [x], 21p. Wrappers.

Based in part on a hitherto unpublished letter of General Nathanael Greene.

5.00

Stone, William C.
The Olivier models. 1969. 19p. Wrappers.

out of print

Thirty-eight ways to take a rare book seriously; a catalogue of original editions of influential books from the Special Collections of Schaffer Library, with commentaries by members of the Union College Faculty. 1982. [44p.] Wrappers.

gratis

THE FOLLOWING ARE DISTRIBUTED BY (BUT WERE NOT ORIGINALLY PUBLISHED BY) THE FRIENDS OF THE UNION COLLEGE LIBRARY:

Somers, Wayne.
Early scientific books in the Schaffer Library, Union College: a checklist. With an introductory essay by Brooke Hindle. (Union College Studies, No.1). 1971. 70p. Wrappers.

Lists, by field, the Library's holdings of pre-1800 scientific books. Includes a printer-place index.

6.00

Union College. Library.
Catalog of that portion of John Bigelow's library not represented by cards in the Library of Congress author catalog. Catalogued by Frances Shaver Smith, assisted by Ruth Anne Evans [&] Helmer Webb. Union College, 1959. 212p. Wrappers.

A full-scale catalog, with title index, of about 2000 of the more unusual books and pamphlets in a library rich in 17th and 18th century French history, philosophy and religious mysticism, in French works on the U.S. Civil War and the French intervention in Mexico, and in Swedenborgiana.

In very short supply 20.00

THE FRIENDS OF THE UNION COLLEGE LIBRARY have published an unusual booklet that may interest many alumni. *Thirty-eight Ways to take a Rare Book Seriously* is the catalogue of an exhibition of original editions of influential books representing most of the fields taught at Union, accompanied by brief essays by members of the faculty.

Selected from the Special Collections of Schaffer Library, the thirty-eight rare books range from the familiar, such as the King James *Bible,* Johnson's *Dictionary* and Hawthorne's *House of the Seven Gables,* through the accessible but less widely read, such as the first full account of the Lewis and Clark expedition, and Admiral Perry's account of the opening of Japan, to volumes now much more easily venerated than perused, such as *Domesday Book* and Isaac Newton's *Principia.*

The catalogue includes essays on each of the books, written for the exhibition by members of the Union faculty.

While supplies last, the Library will gladly mail a complimentary copy of the catalogue to any interested person. To get one, send a postcard to: Friends of the Union College Library, Schaffer Library, Union College, Schenectady, New York 12308. Ask for a copy of *"38 Ways".*

Description: The Friends of the Union College Library has published a variety of materials. Its Publications List is one sheet (11 x 8 1/2"), cream-colored with black print. The individual announcement of Thirty-eight Ways... is a tan card (8 1/2 x 3 7/8") with black print.

"Would it bore you very much reading a MS in a handwriting like mine?": **CATALOGUE**
OF A MEMORIAL EXHIBITION OF THE MSS,
LETTERS, EDITIONS AND MEMORABILIA OF

Joseph Conrad

IN THE EVERETT NEEDHAM CASE LIBRARY
COLGATE UNIVERSITY
HAMILTON, NEW YORK

3 AUGUST 1974 • 30 NOVEMBER 1974

PHILOBIBLON
THE JOURNAL OF
THE FRIENDS OF THE
COLGATE UNIVERSITY LIBRARY
NUMBER 10, SUMMER 1974

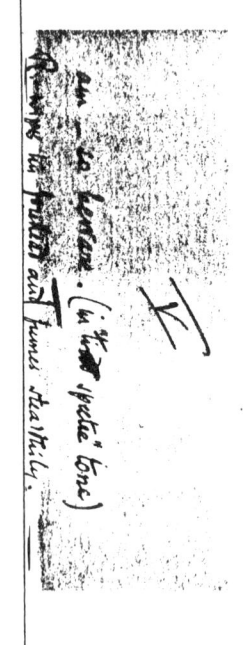

FOREWORD

This exhibition honors the literary achievement of Joseph Conrad. It is also a memorial tribute, opening on the day marking the half-centenary of the author's death and closing on the date of issue of his last complete work of fiction. The forty-one items displayed are drawn from the rich array of Conrad material at Colgate University; and represent no more than ten percent of a body of first and special editions, correspondence, manuscripts, copy, proof, and memorabilia.

This substantial deposit of bibliographical material owes its preservation to the bibliophile Henry A. Colgate, a Trustee of Colgate University from 1916 to 1957. His foundation has been elaborated by gifts from other individuals, and purchases made by The Friends of the Colgate University Library.

J. M. Dent and Sons Ltd. and the Trustees of the Joseph Conrad Estate generously granted permission to reprint and photograph Conrad's text.

Description: The Friends of the Colgate University Library publishes a journal, Philobiblon. The cover and foreword included here are from an exhibition catalogue of a display of Joseph Conrad's manuscripts, letters, editions, and memorabilia. The publication is 9 x 6" and approximately 25 pages.

The Connecticut College Library Bulletin

Number Ten   Summer, 1985

THE CONNECTICUT COLLEGE LIBRARY BULLETIN

Number Ten   *Summer, 1985*

CONTENTS

The Bruce Rogers Collection in the
    Connecticut College Library 3
    Mary R. Kent

Vanderbilt Children's Books 29
    Oliver Jensen

The Legacy of Susanne K. Langer 31
    Brian Rogers

The Connecticut College Library Bulletin is the occasional publication of the Friends of the Library of Connecticut College, Connecticut College, New London, Connecticut, 06320. ISSN 0191-0949.
© Connecticut College. 1985

Description: The Friends of the Connecticut College Library publishes The Connecticut College Library Bulletin on an occasional basis. An example of a cover and contents page of this copyrighted journal is included. The publication is 8 1/2 x 5 1/2" and varies from 25-45 pages in length.

BIBLIOGRAPHY

Bennett, Scott. "Library Friends: A Theoretical History." In *Organizing the Library's Support: Donors, Volunteers, Friends.* Ed. D. W. Krummel. Urbana-Champaign: U of Illinois, 1980. 23-32.

Collins, Rowland. "Friendship and Greatness." *CLIC Quarterly* December (1984): 22-5.

Eaton, Andrew J. "Fund Raising for University Libraries." *College and Research Libraries* 32 (1971): 351-61.

Gwyn, Ann, Anne McArthur, and Karen Furlow. "Friends of the Library." *College and Research Libraries* 36 (1975): 272-82.

Haeuser, Michael. "What Friends Are For: Gaining Financial Independence." *Wilson Library Bulletin* 60 (1986): 25-7.

Holley, Edward G. "The Library and Its Friends." In *Organizing the Library's Support: Donors, Volunteers, Friends.* Ed. D. W. Krummel. Urbana-Champaign: U of Illinois, 1980. 9-22.

SPEC Kit #94. *Fund Raising in ARL Libraries.* Washington: Association of Research Libraries, 1983.